THE BEST OF

CHINESE COOKING

WILLIE MARK

Edited by
John Mitchell

A selection of popular, easy to follow recipes

CENTURION

Contents

The Chinese Kitchen

Introduction

For those not accustomed to Chinese cooking, it may, at first, appear to be extremely difficult and time-consuming, but it should be appreciated that most of the work lies in the initial preparations, while the actual cooking is usually simple, and generally involves little time. Of course there are exceptions, and one or two of the recipes inside may appear complicated at first glance, however I feel sure that with a little patience (and, perhaps, at the beginning, a certain amount of good humour!) all will prove practical. Home cooked Chinese meals most often consist of several dishes served simultaneously, and usually allow for one main course per person, with a soup, and a rice or noodle dish, being served in addition. However one of the delights of serving Chinese food, is the flexibility offered, so that personal tastes and preferences become all important, and the number and order of dishes, may be altered at will, with quantities adjusted accordingly. For this reason it was not considered practical to indicate a number of servings for each recipe. I feel sure that with just a little experimenting, and perhaps a small amount of improvisation (an essential ingredient in any good kitchen) excellent results will be achieved.

INGREDIENTS

The recipes have been edited so that it is unlikely that any ingredient will prove too difficult to obtain outside Asia. Certainly, some items may not be found in the village or suburban shop but they should all be available in city supermarkets or Chinese produce stores. Many of the recipes call for the use of Chinese wine and if cooking is planned only for rare occasions it may be more economical to substitute a medium-dry sherry.

RICE

Rice is a staple food for a large proportion of the world's population and is an essential part of a Chinese meal. At the family table a steaming bowl of rice will take pride of place in the centre to be enjoyed by all throughout the meal but on more formal occasions it will usually be served towards the end of the meal. The important thing to ensure is that, steamed, boiled or fried, it's light, fluffy and cooked to perfection.

CHOPSTICKS

The use of knives, forks and spoons should not in reality detract from the pleasure of eating well cooked Chinese food and yet most people who have once mastered the art of using chopsticks will agree that it seems to. The first time you try using chopsticks it may seem awkward and difficult but with a little persistence you'll be an expert. Start by gripping one of the chopsticks in a fixed and firm position in the right hand (see illustrations below), then take the second one between the thumb and forefinger and manipulate it as you would a pencil. In no time at all you'll be picking up the smallest morsels with ease and will in the process add greatly to the enjoyment of your Chinese meal.

Fried Rice in any one of its many and varied combinations may be served as part of a multi-course meal or as a simple but satisfying dish.

WEIGHTS & MEASURES

The recipes were written using metric measurements and the Imperial alternatives (bracketed) have been rounded up or down to serve as a practical rather than a precise guide. Measurements over 75 grams (75g) or 75 millilitres (75ml) are shown in units of 25 and below that in 5g teaspoons (tsp) or 15g tablespoons (Tbsp). However, I would stress that Asian cooks tend not to be as dependent on scales and measuring cups as are many of their western counterparts and with any recipe, and in particular where spicy dishes are concerned, the best results to suit personal tastes will only come from some experimentation.

EQUIPMENT

While a well-equipped western kitchen will include everything necessary to prepare a complete and delicious Chinese meal there is no doubt that certain items designed for specific purposes will make life easier and cooking more fun. Certainly, where the intention is to cook Chinese (or other Asian) food quite frequently the early purchase of a wok, that most versatile and practical round-based cooking pan, is highly recommended. Make sure it has a tightly-fitting lid and, at the same time, purchase a bamboo rack to fit inside. After that, a set of bamboo steaming baskets, a pair of long chopsticks and a very sharp cleaver (or knife) should provide all the additional equipment you require. Having said that, however, I should add that the use of your heavy-based frying pans and saucepans will prove quite satisfactory for the preparation of the following recipes.

Dim Sum

For breakfast, lunch and afternoon tea many Chinese restaurants feature *Dim Sum*, a seemingly endless variety of small dishes, very often served in the traditional manner by girls carrying trays or pushing carts and calling out the names of the various dishes as they weave their way through crowded tables. Because a *'Dim Sum'* meal depends so much on a wide selection of dishes it is not always practical to serve at home. However, individual items can make delicious snacks or, if serving a meal in the Western style, ideal 'starters'.

Spring Rolls

SPRING ROLLS

2 dried Chinese mushrooms
175 g (6 oz) bean sprouts
125 g (4 oz) bamboo shoot
125 g (4 oz) roasted pork
125 g (4 oz) fresh shrimps
oil for deep-frying
2 Tbsp Chinese wine
1 Tbsp light soya sauce
1 tsp dark soya sauce
1/2 tsp sesame oil
2 tsp sugar
1/4 tsp white pepper
1 Tbsp cornflour
12 spring roll wrappers
egg-wash

Soak the mushrooms in warm water for 30 minutes, then discard the hard stems. Blanch the bean sprouts. Cut the mushroom caps, bamboo shoot and pork into fine shreds. Shell and de-vein the shrimps and chop finely. Heat 4 Tbsp of oil in a wok, add the mushroom and bamboo shoot and stir-fry over a high heat for 1 minute. Add the bean sprouts, pork and shrimp and cook for 1 minute, then add the wine, soya sauce, sesame oil, sugar and pepper and continue cooking for a further minute, stirring frequently. Mix the cornflour with a small quantity of cold water and stir into the mixture, then remove from the heat and allow to cool. Lay the wrappers on a lightly-greased surface and spoon a portion of the mixture on to the centre of each.

Fold one corner of the wrapper over the filling, fold in each side and roll up tightly, then press the ends to seal and brush with the egg-wash. Heat the remaining oil in a large wok until it is very hot (almost smoking), then reduce to a moderate heat and deep-fry the rolls until golden brown and crispy. Drain on kitchen paper and serve immediately.

FRIED TARO DUMPLINGS

450 g (1 lb) taro
3 dried Chinese mushrooms
125 g (4 oz) fresh shrimps
125 g (4 oz) lean pork
vegetable oil for frying
2 tsp cornflour
salt to taste
freshly ground black pepper
3 Tbsp plain flour
75 g (3 oz) melted lard

Peel and cut the taros into slices. Place in a steamer and cook until tender, then mash while still hot. Soak the mushrooms in warm water for 30 minutes, discard the hard stems and dice the caps. Shell and de-vein the shrimps and chop finely. Chop the pork finely. Heat 2 Tbsp of oil in a pan and stir-fry the pork and shrimp for 2 minutes. Mix the cornflour with a little cold water and add to the pan. Season to taste with salt and freshly ground black pepper and continue to cook for a further 2 minutes, then remove and drain on kitchen paper. Sift the flour into a mixing bowl, add the lard, a pinch of salt and the mashed taro and knead well. Turn on to a lightly-floured surface and shape into a roll. Cut into slices, place the shrimp and pork mixture into the centres and fold. Pinch the edges with the fingers and seal with a little water. Heat the remaining oil in a large pan and deep-fry the taro dumplings until crispy and golden brown. Serve immediately.

ONION CAKES

6 spring onions
250 g (9 oz) plain flour
75 g (3 oz) melted lard
1/2 tsp salt
1/4 tsp white pepper
1/4 tsp Chinese five-spice powder
2 Tbsp sesame oil
egg-wash
oil for deep-frying

Chop the spring onions into tiny pieces. Sift the flour into a mixing bowl and add just sufficient boiling water to produce a thick, sticky dough, then add the melted lard, salt, pepper, five-spice powder and half the sesame oil and knead until smooth. Then, roll out on a lightly-floured surface and cover evenly with the chopped spring onion. Sprinkle the remaining sesame oil on top and shape the dough into a roll approximately 50 mm (2 inches) in diameter. Divide into 20 mm (3/4 inch) slices, flatten slightly and brush with the egg-wash. Heat the oil in a wok until it starts to smoke, then lower heat and deep-fry the onion cakes until the outsides are crispy and golden brown.

STEAMED PRAWN DUMPLINGS

16 won ton wrappers
450 g (1 lb) prawns
2 dried Chinese mushrooms
75 g (3 oz) fat pork
2 tinned water chestnuts
2 spring onions
2 Tbsp chopped bamboo shoot
1 Tbsp Chinese wine
2 tsp light soya sauce
1 tsp dark soya sauce
2 tsp sesame oil
freshly ground black pepper
egg-wash

Spread out the won ton wrappers on a flat, cold, lightly-greased surface. Shell and de-vein the prawns. Soak the mushrooms in warm water for 30 minutes, then discard the hard stems. Finely chop the prawns, pork, mushrooms, water chestnuts, spring onions and bamboo shoot and place in a mixing bowl. Add the wine, soya sauce, sesame oil and pepper and mix well. Spoon portions of the mixture onto the wrappers, fold into small dumplings and crimp at the top. Brush with the egg-wash and place on a rack. Place the rack in a wok, cover with a tightly-fitting lid and cook over rapidly boiling water for 10-12 minutes.

SHRIMP TOAST & SESAME SEEDS

450 g (1 lb) shrimps
1 clove garlic
1 egg-white
2 tsp light soya sauce
2 tsp cornflour
1/2 tsp salt
1/2 tsp white pepper
8 slices white bread
2 Tbsp sesame seeds
oil for deep-frying

Shell and de-vein the shrimps and chop very finely. Crush the garlic. Beat the egg-white in a bowl and add the shrimp, garlic, soya sauce, cornflour, salt and pepper and mix well to form a thick, smooth paste. Cut the crusts off the bread, spread the mixture on evenly and sprinkle with sesame seeds. Heat the oil in a wok until it starts to smoke, then lower heat and deep-fry the pieces of bread until golden. Remove with a slotted spoon, drain off all excess oil and cut into squares.

Dim Sum Selection

STEAMED MEAT BALLS

300 g (10 oz) minced beef
2 water chestnuts
1 shallot
1 spring onion
20 mm (³/4 inch) fresh ginger
1 tsp chopped coriander
1 tsp sesame oil
1 Tbsp cornflour
salt to taste
freshly ground black pepper

Pound the meat until it becomes a smooth paste. Chop the water chestnuts, shallot, spring onion and ginger very finely and combine with the meat. Add the coriander, sesame oil, cornflour, salt, pepper and 2 Tbsp of water and mix to blend thoroughly. Shape the mixture into balls about 25 mm (1 inch) in diameter and arrange on a heatproof plate. Place in a steamer and cook over rapidly boiling water for 10-15 minutes, then serve immediately.

MANDARIN BEEF

300 g (10 oz) lean beef steak
¹/2 tsp salt
¹/2tsp black pepper
2 eggs
2 tsp cornflour
1 Tbsp chopped dried
mandarin peel
15 mm (³/4 inch) knob fresh ginger
2 fresh red chillies
2 spring onions
oil for deep-frying
1 Tbsp sugar
1 tsp dark soya sauce
1 Tbsp light soya sauce
2 Tbsp Chinese wine
2 Tbsp beef stock
1 tsp sesame oil

Cut the beef into small thin slices and season with salt and pepper. Beat the eggs, mix with the cornflour and pour over the beef, then set aside for 20 minutes. Soak the mandarin peel in ginger, chillies and spring onion. Heat half the oil in a wok until it starts to smoke, add the beef and stir-fry for 2-3 minutes, then remove and drain on kitchen paper. Clean the pan, heat the remaining oil and the ginger, chilli, spring onions and mandarin peel and stir-fry for 1 minute. Then add sugar, soya sauce, wine and stock and bring to the boil. Continue to cook until the liquid has almost completely reduced, then return the beef to the pan, adjust seasonings to taste and continue to cook for a further 2-3 minutes, stirring frequently. Finally, transfer to a serving dish and sprinkle with sesame oil.

BARBECUED PORK

900 g (2 lb) boned pork loin
with skin
2 cloves garlic
20 mm (³/4 inch) knob fresh ginger
4 Tbsp Chinese wine
4 Tbsp light soya sauce
3 Tbsp sugar
¹/4 tsp red food colouring
2 tsp salt
75 g (3 oz) clear honey

Score the skin of the pork with a sharp knife and cut into strips, approximately 40 mm (1¹/2 inches) wide. Chop the garlic and ginger very finely and combine with the wine, soya sauce, sugar and food colouring. Rub the mixture into the underside of the pork and rub the salt into the scored skin. Set aside for 30 minutes, then thread the meat on a spit and coat with a little honey. Cook over hot charcoals for 25-35 minutes, turning at frequent intervals and basting with the honey. When the meat is cooked coat with the remaining honey and cut into thin slices.

FRIED MEAT DUMPLINGS

2 dried Chinese mushrooms
250 g (9 oz) pork
½ tsp minced garlic
2 Tbsp finely chopped
bamboo shoot
2 Tbsp finely chopped spring onion
oil for deep-frying
1 Tbsp Chinese wine
2 tsp light soya sauce
1 tsp sesame oil
1 tsp sugar
salt to taste
freshly ground white pepper
12 won ton wrappers
egg-wash

Soak the mushrooms in warm water for 30 minutes, then discard the hard stems and chop the caps very finely. Pass the pork through a fine mincer. Heat 3 Tbsp of oil in a wok and stir-fry the meat, vegetables and garlic for 2 minutes. Add the wine, soya sauce, sesame oil, sugar, salt and pepper and continue to cook for a further 2 minutes, stirring frequently. Remove the mixture from the pan, drain on kitchen paper and allow to cook. Lay the wrappers on a lightly-greased surface and spoon a small portion of mixture on to each one, then fold into triangle shapes and brush with the egg-wash. Heat the remaining oil in a clean wok and deep-fry the dumplings until golden brown and crispy.

STEAMED BUNS WITH PORK FILLING

225 g (8 oz) roasted pork
3 spring onions
2 Tbsp vegetable oil
4 Tbsp oyster sauce
2 Tbsp light soya sauce
2 tsp sugar
2 Tbsp chicken stock
freshly ground black pepper
1 Tbsp cornflour

Dough:
2 Tbsp sugar
1 Tbsp dried yeast
450 g (1 lb) plain flour
¼ tsp salt

Cut the pork into small, thin slices and finely chop the spring onions. Heat the oil in a pan, add the onion and stir-fry for 1 minute, then add the pork, oyster sauce, soya sauce, sugar, pepper and chicken stock and cook over a moderate heat for 2-3 minutes, stirring occasionally. Mix the cornflour with a small quantity of cold water and add to the pork. Stir well, then remove from the heat and allow to cool. Spoon small quantities of pork on to the dough pieces and fold up the edges to form buns, leaving small openings at the top. Place the buns in a steamer and cook over rapidly boiling water for 10-12 minutes.

To make the dough; dissolve the sugar in 100 ml (4 fl oz) of warm water, stir in the yeast and allow to ferment for 10 minutes. Sift the flour and salt into a mixing bowl, make a well in the centre and gradually add the fermented yeast. Mix with a wooden spoon, then knead firmly for 10 minutes. Turn out on to a lightly-floured surface and shape into a roll, approximately 50 mm (2 inches) in diameter, then cut into 25 mm (1 inch) slices and flatten with the hands.

Soups

Soup is an important part of a Chinese meal and will nearly always be served, both at home and in restaurants. At formal dinners, or banquets, it will often be served twice; a thick, substantial soup being served halfway through the meal with a light clear broth towards the end, to clear the palate for a final sweet course. Two of the most popular ingredients for special soups are Shark's Fin and Bird's Nest and, while neither is common to any Western cuisine, both are readily available in dried form. In the winter months many Chinese restaurants feature Snake Soup, which is said to be beneficial to one's general well-being.

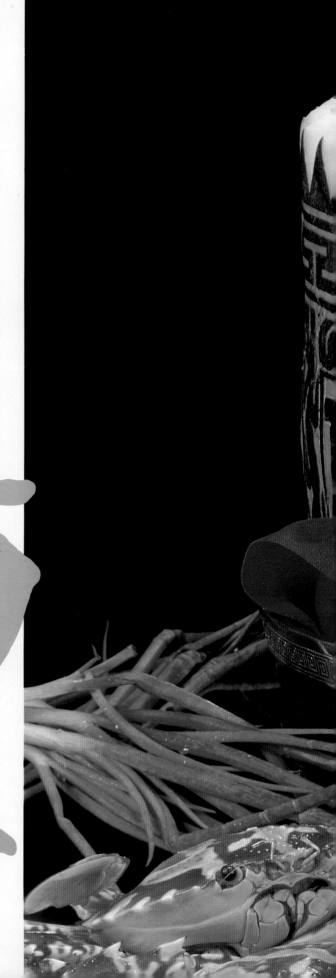

Winter Melon Soup

WINTER MELON SOUP

1 large winter melon
6 dried Chinese mushrooms
4 tinned water chestnuts
75 g (3 oz) shrimps
75 g (3 oz) crabmeat
100 g (4 oz) lean pork
100 g (4 oz) chicken meat
75 g (3 oz) duck meat
1 Tbsp chopped Yunnan ham
1 spring onion
1 clove garlic
20 mm (3/4 inch) knob fresh ginger
1.5 litres (2½ pints) chicken stock
salt to taste
freshly ground black pepper
1 tsp dark soya sauce
½ tsp sesame oil

Remove the top quarter of the melon and cut the base so the melon will stand upright. Carefully scoop out the seeds and sufficient pulp to allow the stock to be poured in, taking care not to break the skin. Soak the mushrooms in warm water for 30 minutes and discard the hard stems. Cut the mushrooms into strips. Peel the water chestnuts and chop finely. Shell and de-vein the shrimps and flake the crabmeat. Dice the pork, chicken, duck and ham and blanch in boiling water for 1 minute, then pat dry. Finely chop the spring onion, garlic and ginger. Pour the stock into a large pan and bring to the boil, then add the mushroom, chestnut, pork, chicken, duck, ham, onion, garlic and ginger. Season to taste with salt and pepper, simmer for 15 minutes, then pour into the melon. Place the melon in a steamer, cover it with its own 'lid', then cover the pan. Cook gently for approximately 4 hours, then add the shrimp, crabmeat, soya sauce and sesame oil and continue to cook for a further 30 minutes. To serve: scoop out the flesh of the melon and place in individual bowls and top up with stock.

HOT & SOUR SOUP

4 dried Chinese mushrooms
75 g (3 oz) bamboo shoot
75 g (3 oz) cucumber
2 fresh red chillies
20 mm (3/4 inch) knob fresh ginger
75 g (3 oz) beancurd
125 g (4 oz) fresh shrimps
125 g (4 oz) roasted pork
2 Tbsp vegetable oil
1.75 litres (3 pints) chicken stock
2 tsp light soya sauce
2 tsp dark soya sauce
1 Tbsp Chinese wine
1 Tbsp vinegar
1 tsp white pepper
2 tsp cornflour
1 egg
1 tsp chilli oil

Soak the mushrooms in warm water for 30 minutes, then discard the hard stems and shred the caps. Shred the bamboo shoot, cucumber, chillies and ginger and cut the beancurd into small dice. Shell and de-vein the shrimps and cut in half lengthways. Shred the pork. Heat the oil in a pan, add all the above and stir-fry for 2 minutes, then pour in the stock and bring to the boil. Add the soya sauce, wine, vinegar and pepper and stir well. Lower the heat and allow to simmer for 3 minutes. Mix the cornflour with a small quantity of cold water and add to the soup to thicken slightly. Whisk the egg lightly and stir into the soup for 30 seconds, then transfer to a tureen. Finally, heat the chilli oil and sprinkle this over the soup.

MUSHROOM & CRISPY RICE SOUP

8 dried Chinese mushrooms
200 g (7 oz) glutenous rice
1.5 litres (2½ pints) chicken stock
2 Tbsp Chinese wine
1 tsp dark soya sauce
½ tsp salt
¼ tsp white pepper
oil for deep-frying
1 tsp chopped coriander

Place the mushrooms in a shallow dish and pour in sufficient warm water to cover. Allow to soak for 30 minutes, then remove and discard the hard stems but retain the water. Slice the mushroom caps. Steam the rice in a large pan until it is overcooked and sticks to the bottom of the pan. Allow to cool slightly, then remove carefully and cut into bite-size pieces. Pour the stock into a large saucepan and bring to the boil. Add the mushrooms, reserved water, Chinese wine, soya sauce, salt and freshly ground white pepper. Boil rapidly for 2 minutes, then lower the heat and simmer for 35 minutes. Meanwhile, heat the oil in a wok and deep-fry the pieces of rice until they are crispy and golden. To serve; place the pieces of rice in a soup tureen and pour the boiling soup on top. Garnish with chopped coriander.

BIRD'S NEST & QUAIL EGG SOUP

75 g (3 oz) dried bird's nest
1 Tbsp Chinese wine
1 Tbsp light soya sauce
1.5 litres (2½ pints) chicken stock
2 spring onions
75 g (3 oz) snow peas
salt to taste
freshly ground black pepper
12 quail eggs
1 Tbsp finely shredded ham

Soak the bird's nest in cold water for 4 hours, then drain, carefully remove any impurities and place in a saucepan. Cover with cold water and bring to the boil, then reduce heat, add the wine and soya sauce and simmer for 30 minutes. Drain and set aside. Bring the stock to the boil and season to taste with salt and pepper. Cut the spring onions into short lengths and add to the stock together with the snow peas. Reduce the heat and simmer for 5 minutes, then add the bird's nest and continue to cook over a moderate heat for a further 2-3 minutes. Meanwhile, break the eggs into small dishes, top each with a little shredded ham and poach until set. To serve; pour the soup into a tureen and float the poached eggs on top.

SEAFOOD & BEANCURD SOUP

75 g (3 oz) shrimps
75 g (3 oz) cooked crabmeat
1 egg
2 tsp light soya sauce
1 tsp sesame oil
2 Tbsp cornflour
freshly ground black pepper
225 g (8 oz) fresh beancurd
1 spring onion
15 mm (1/2 inch) knob fresh ginger
1.5 litres (2 1/2 pints) chicken stock
salt to taste
1 Tbsp Chinese wine
2 tsp chopped coriander

Shell and de-vein the shrimps and flake the crabmeat. Break the egg into a bowl, add the soya sauce, sesame oil, 2 tsp cornflour and pepper and mix well. Coat the shrimps with half the mixture and the crabmeat with the remainder and set both aside for 30 minutes. Chop the beancurd and spring onion and shred the ginger. Pour the stock into a large pan and bring to the boil, then add the beancurd and ginger and season with salt to taste. Allow to boil rapidly for 1 minute, then add the shrimps, crabmeat and spring onion, bring back to the boil and stir well. Mix the remaining cornflour with a little cold water and stir into the soup to thicken slightly. Transfer to a tureen, stir in the wine and garnish with chopped coriander.

CRABMEAT & SWEET CORN SOUP

250g (9 oz) cooked crabmeat
2 Tbsp Chinese wine
1 tsp sesame oil
salt to taste
freshly ground black pepper
2 tsp cornflour
1.25 litres (2 pints) chicken stock
275 g (10 oz) tinned sweet corn
2 Tbsp cornflour
2 eggs
2 Tbsp finely chopped ham
1 tsp chopped coriander

Flake the crabmeat and place in a shallow dish. Mix the wine with the sesame oil, salt, pepper and half the cornflour and pour onto the crab, then set aside for 15 minutes. Pour the chicken stock into a saucepan, add the sweet corn and bring slowly to the boil. Lower the heat and allow to simmer for 2-3 minutes, then add the crabmeat, bring back to the boil and cook for a further minute. Mix the remaining cornflour with a small quantity of cold water and add to the soup to thicken slightly. Whisk the eggs lightly and pour into the soup, stirring continuously until the egg starts to set in threads, then transfer to a tureen and garnish with chopped ham and coriander.

SHARK'S FIN SOUP WITH ABALONE

250 g (9 oz) dried shark's fin
75 g (3 oz) Yunnan ham
100 g (4 oz) fresh chicken meat
4 spring onions
25 mm (1 inch) knob fresh ginger
1.5 (2½ pints) chicken stock
2 Tbsp Chinese wine
2 Tbsp light soya sauce
2 tsp dark soya sauce
salt to taste
freshly ground black pepper
150 g (5 oz) tinned abalone
2 Tbsp vegetable oil
finely chopped fresh coriander

Place the shark's fin in a large saucepan, cover with cold water and soak overnight. Drain thoroughly, then place back in the pan, cover with fresh water and bring to the boil. Lower heat and simmer for about 2 hours, then rinse under cold running water for 5 minutes. (To test if the shark's fin is ready for steaming, press gently between the fingers and it should break easily. If it fails to do so, cover with fresh water, bring back to the boil and continue to simmer for a further period, then test again). Meanwhile, shred the ham and chicken meat and chop finely the spring onions and ginger. Pour the stock into a double-boiler and bring to the boil. Add the shark's fin, ham, chicken, spring onion, ginger, Chinese wine, soya sauce, salt and pepper and cover with a tightly fitting lid. Place over boiling water and steam for 2-3 hours. Finally, cut the abalone into thin slices and stir-fry in hot oil for 1 minute. To serve; divide the shark's fin into individual bowls, add a few slices of abalone and pour the boiling stock on top. Garnish with finely chopped fresh coriander.

ABALONE & VEGETABLE SOUP

300 g (10 oz) canned abalone
4 dried Chinese mushrooms
2 carrots
6 long green beans
15 mm (¾ inch) knob fresh ginger
1 clove garlic
2 Tbsp vegetable oil
1.5 litres (2½ pints) chicken stock
100 g (4 oz) button mushrooms
100 g (4 oz) straw mushrooms
2 tsp dark soya sauce
1 Tbsp Chinese wine
salt to taste
freshly ground white pepper

Cut the abalone into thin slices. Soak the dried mushrooms in warm water for 40 minutes, then discard the stems and slice the caps. Slice the carrots and cut the beans into 25 mm (1 inch) lengths. Finely chop the ginger and crush the garlic. Heat the oil in a pan and stir-fry the ginger and garlic for 2 minutes, then add the carrots, beans, soya sauce and wine and cook for a further minute. Season to taste with salt and pepper, then lower the heat, cover the pan and allow to simmer for 3-4 minutes.

SHREDDED BEEF SOUP

300 g (10 oz) lean beef
3 egg-whites
1 tsp cornflour
1/4 tsp salt
1/4 tsp white pepper
2 tsp sugar
2 Tbsp Chinese wine
1 Tbsp light soya sauce
1 tsp sesame oil
1.5 litres (2 1/2 pints) stock
2 tsp finely chopped spring onion
1 tsp finely chopped coriander

Shred the beef and place in a shallow dish. Mix one egg-white with the cornflour, salt, pepper, sugar, wine, soya sauce and sesame oil and pour over the beef. Allow to stand for 20 minutes, then strain and retain the marinade. Pour water into a saucepan and bring to the boil, then add the beef and bring back to the boil. Cook for 2 minutes, then remove the beef with a slotted spoon and pour away the water. Add the stock to the pan and bring to the boil, then add the reserved marinade. Lightly whisk the remaining egg-white and stir into the soup, then replace the beef and cook for a further minute. Finally, transfer to a tureen and sprinkle the finely chopped spring onion and coriander on top.

PORK LIVER & TOMATO SOUP

175 g (6 oz) pork liver
3 large tomatoes
1 spring onion
20 mm (3/4 inch) knob fresh ginger
1 Tbsp light soya sauce
2 tsp dark soya sauce
2 tsp sugar
1 Tbsp cornflour
1.5 litres (2 1/2 pints) chicken stock
2 Tbsp vegetable oil
2 tsp Chinese wine
freshly ground black pepper

Cut the liver into small thin pieces and soak in cold water for 30 minutes. Remove and dry on kitchen paper. Cut the tomatoes into thin slices and chop the spring onion and ginger. Mix together the soya sauce, sugar, cornflour and 2 Tbsp of cold water, add the onion, ginger and liver and toss to coat evenly. Set aside for 30 minutes. Pour the stock into a large pan and bring to a rapid boil, then add the tomatoes, lower heat and simmer for 10 minutes. Meanwhile, heat the oil in a wok, add the liver together with the marinade and stir-fry for 2-3 minutes. Remove liver from the oil and drain on kitchen paper, then add to the stock and continue to cook over a moderate heat for a further 2 minutes. Finally, stir in the wine, season to taste with pepper and transfer to a soup tureen.

Seafoods

China's coastal waters abound with a rich variety of seafood and picturesque fishing junks in full sail can be seen each and every day of the year bringing in their catches to satisfy the demand of the housewife and professional chef alike for absolute freshness. Fish is often taken home from the market in a plastic bag of water and only killed immediately prior to cooking and, likewise many of the excellent seafood restaurants which are to be found throughout the country offer the opportunity of selecting directly from a live-fish tank.

Chiu Chow Cold Lobster

CHIU CHOW COLD LOBSTER

1 fresh lobster, approx 1 kilo
(2¼ lbs)
½ tsp salt
10 black peppercorns
100 g (4 oz) thinly sliced Yunnan
ham
cucumber slices
sprigs of fresh coriander
tangerine jam dip

Tie the lobster to a board (to keep in a straight position) and plunge into a pan of boiling salted water. Add the peppercorns and cook for 10-12 minutes, then remove from the pan and allow to cool. Break off the claws and tail and remove all the meat. Thoroughly clean the back shell and place in a refrigerator with the meat for 30 minutes. Remove, slice the meat and arrange in the shell with alternating layers of ham. Garnish with slices of cucumber and sprigs of fresh coriander. Serve with a tangerine jam dip.

LOBSTER WITH CHINESE WINE

1 fresh medium-size lobster
2 tsp vinegar
1 tsp salt
½ tsp white pepper
2 brown onions
1 clove garlic
oil for deep-frying
225 ml (8 fl oz) clear fish stock
2 Tbsp sugar
3 Tbsp Chinese wine
1 tsp dark soya sauce
2 Tbsp tomato sauce
2 tsp cornflour
1 tsp finely-chopped coriander

Place the lobster into a pan of rapidly boiling water, add the vinegar and cook for 15-20 minutes. Then, remove, discard the head and tail and chop the body of the lobster into 16 pieces. Season with salt and pepper. Chop the onion and crush the garlic. Heat the oil in a wok until it starts to smoke, then add the lobster and deep-fry for 1 minute. Remove with a slotted spoon, drain off all excess oil and set aside. Pour away most of the oil from the wok. Reheat, add the onion and garlic and stir-fry for 1 minute. Then, pour in the stock and bring to the boil. Add the sugar, wine, soya sauce, tomato sauce and stir well. Replace the lobster, adjust seasonings to taste and cook over a medium heat for 2 minutes. Finally, mix the cornflour with a small quantity of cold water and stir into the sauce to thicken slightly. Transfer to a serving dish and sprinkle the finely-chopped coriander on top.

STIR-FRIED LOBSTER

1 large fresh lobster
1 tsp cornflour
¹/₂ tsp salt
¹/₄ tsp white pepper
25mm (1 inch) knob fresh ginger
2 spring onions
1 small green pepper
1 clove garlic
150ml (6 fl oz) peanut oil
2 Tbsp Chinese wine
2 tsp light soya sauce
1 tsp sugar
225ml (8 fl oz) clear fish stock
fresh parsley sprigs

Place the lobster into a pan of rapidly boiling water. Immediately bring the water back to the boil and cook allowing 5-6 minutes per 450g (1 lb). Allow to cool, then remove the meat and cut into bite-sized chunks. Sprinkle the cornflour over the meat and season with salt and pepper. Chop finely the ginger, spring onions and green pepper and crush the garlic. Heat the oil in a wok and stir-fry the lobster for 1 minute, then remove and pour away most of the oil. Add the ginger and garlic to the remaining oil and stir-fry for 3 minutes, then add the spring onion and green pepper and replace the lobster. Stir-fry for a further minute then add the wine, soya sauce, sugar and stock and bring to the boil. Lower the heat, adjust seasonings to taste and cook slowly for another 2 minutes, then transfer to a serving plate and garnish with sprigs of fresh parsley.

DEEP-FRIED CRAB CLAWS

8 fresh crab claws
150 g (5 oz) fresh shrimps
75 g (3 oz) fat pork
1 egg-white
1 tsp sugar
¼ tsp salt
¼ tsp white pepper
2 tsp light soya sauce
1 tsp dark soya sauce
1 tsp sesame oil
2 Tbsp cornflour
vegetable oil for deep-frying

Crack the claws and cook in a steamer for 10 minutes. Carefully remove the shell, leaving the claw meat intact and still attached to the 'nipper'. Shell and de-vein the shrimps and place through a mincer, together with the pork. In a bowl, beat the egg-white lightly then add the minced shrimp, sugar, salt, pepper, soya sauce, sesame oil and half the cornflour and blend well until the mixture becomes sticky, adding a little cold water if necessary. Then, mould the mixture around each crab claw and dust with the remaining cornflour. To cook; heat the vegetable oil in a wok until it starts to smoke, then deep-fry the crab claws until the outside is crispy and golden. Drain thoroughly before serving.

CRABMEAT OMELETTE

300 g (10 oz) cooked crabmeat
¼ tsp salt
¼ tsp white pepper
1 small green pepper
2 spring onions
15 mm (½ inch) knob fresh ginger
1 clove garlic
3 Tbsp peanut oil
1 Tbsp Chinese wine
2 tsp light soya sauce
6 eggs
1 tsp finely chopped coriander
1 tsp sesame oil

Flake the crabmeat and season with salt and pepper. Chop the green pepper and spring onions very finely and mince the ginger and garlic. Heat half the peanut oil in a large frying pan, add the green pepper, onion, ginger and garlic and stir-fry over a moderate heat for 2 minutes, then add the crabmeat, wine and soya sauce and stir well. Cook for a further minute, then remove and drain off excess oil. Clean the pan, add remaining peanut oil and place over a moderate heat. Break the eggs into a large bowl, whisk lightly, then add the coriander, sesame oil and crab mixture, stir to blend and pour into the pan. Lower heat immediately and cook slowly, turning once, until the egg is set.

CRAB WITH PORK & EGG

2 medium sized crabs
1 tsp salt
2 Tbsp vinegar
6 thin slices cooked pork
4 eggs
3 shallots
2 spring onions
25mm (1 inch) knob fresh ginger
2 cloves garlic
2 Tbsp fermented black beans
1 tsp finely chopped dried orange
peel
2 Tbsp Chinese wine
2 Tbsp light soya sauce
freshly ground black pepper
2 Tbsp white breadcrumbs
2 tsp sesame oil

Clean the crabs and place in a pan of rapidly-boiling water. Add the vinegar and salt and cook for 15-20 minutes. Carefully remove all the meat (and any coral) from the bodies and the claws and place in a shallow heat-proof dish. Retain the crab shells and claws. Cover the crab meat with pieces of pork. Break the eggs into a mixing bowl and beat lightly. Chop finely the shallots, spring onion and ginger and crush the garlic and add these to the beaten egg. Then, add the soya beans, orange peel, wine and soya sauce and pepper. Blend thoroughly and pour over the crab and pork. Place the dish on a bamboo rack arranged inside a wok. Pour in a small amount of boiling water, cover the wok with a tightly-fitting lid and steam for 20 minutes. Then, transfer the mixture to an earthenware casserole dish, cover with breadcrumbs and sprinkle the sesame oil on top. Bake in a pre-heated moderate oven for 10 minutes, then decorate with the crab claws and shells.

BAKED STUFFED CRAB SHELLS

1 fresh crab, approx 550 g (1¹/₄ lb)
¹/₂ tsp white pepper
1 egg
2 dried Chinese mushrooms
100 g (4 oz) fresh prawns
1 small brown onion
1 spring onion
1 Tbsp chopped chicken liver
75 ml (3 fl oz) peanut oil
2 tsp cornflour
2 Tbsp chicken stock
2 Tbsp light soya sauce
2 Tbsp bread crumbs

Steam the crab over rapidly boiling water for 15 minutes, then carefully lift off the top shell and extract all the meat from the body and claws. Wash the shell and place in a warming oven. Flake the crabmeat, place in a shallow dish and season with pepper. Whisk the egg lightly and pour over the crabmeat and set aside for 30 minutes. Soak the mushrooms in warm water for 30 minutes and discard the hard stems. Shell and de-vein the prawns. Chop finely the mushroom caps, prawns, onion and spring onion. Heat the oil in a wok and stir-fry the onion and spring onion for 2 minutes, then add the mushroom, crabmeat, prawn and chicken liver and continue to stir-fry for a further 2 minutes. Mix the cornflour with a small quantity of stock and add the remaining stock and soya sauce to the wok. Bring to the boil, then lower heat and stir in the cornflour. Mix well for 30 seconds, then spoon the mixture into the crab shell and sprinkle the bread crumbs on top. Bake in a moderately-hot oven for 6-8 minutes until the top is golden.

BRAISED CRAB WITH GINGER

2 fresh crabs
3 Tbsp cornflour
25 mm (1 inch) knob fresh ginger
2 shallots
2 spring onions
oil for deep frying
225 ml (8 fl oz) chicken stock
2 Tbsp Chinese wine
2 tsp dark soya sauce
2 tsp sesame oil
1 tsp sugar
salt to taste
freshly ground black pepper

Prepare the crabs, chop into serving-size pieces and dust with half the cornflour. Grate the ginger and chop finely the shallots and spring onions. Heat the oil in a wok and deep-fry the crab pieces for 2 minutes, then remove and pour away most of the oil. Add the ginger, shallots and spring onion to the wok and stir-fry for 1 minute, then add the stock, wine, soya sauce, sesame oil, sugar, salt and pepper and bring to the boil. Replace the crab, cover the wok with a tightly-fitting lid and continue to cook over a moderate heat until the crab is fully cooked, approximately 6-8 minutes. Finally, mix the remaining cornflour with a small quantity of cold water and stir into the sauce until it thickens slightly.

PRAWNS WITH BLACK BEANS

450 g (1 lb) fresh prawns
2 Tbsp fermented black beans
3 cloves garlic
1 fresh red chilli
2 spring onions
2 Tbsp Chinese wine
1 tsp sugar
¼ tsp salt
¼ tsp white pepper
2 Tbsp peanut oil
1 tsp sesame oil

Shell and de-vein the prawns, leaving the tails intact, and place in a shallow dish. Place the black beans in a bowl and mash with a fork. Crush the garlic and chop finely the chilli and spring onions, then add to the beans, together with the wine, sugar, salt and pepper. Blend thoroughly and spread over the prawns. Place the dish in a steamer and cook over rapidly boiling water for 5-6 minutes. Heat the peanut oil and sesame oil until almost smoking, then pour over the prawns and serve immediately.

PRAWNS WITH SPRING ONIONS

575 g (1¼ lbs) prawns
2 spring onions
2 cloves garlic
125 ml (4 fl oz) peanut oil

Sauce:
3 Tbsp light soya sauce
1 Tbsp Chinese wine
1 tsp sesame oil
150 ml (5 fl oz) chicken stock
1 tsp sugar
freshly ground white pepper
2 tsp cornflour

Slit the prawns down the back and remove the vein, leaving the shells attached, then arrange side by side on a heatproof plate. Chop the spring onions and garlic. Place the prawns in a steamer and cook over rapidly boiling water for 3-4 minutes, then remove, drain off any liquid and keep warm. Heat the oil in a small pan, add the garlic and stir until well browned. Then, discard the garlic and pour the flavoured oil over the prawns. Sprinkle the spring onion on top and cover with the sauce.

To make the sauce: mix all the ingredients, place in a pan and bring to the boil. Then, lower heat and allow to simmer for 2 minutes, stirring frequently.

STEAMED PRAWNS

675g (1½ lbs) fresh king prawns
25mm (1 inch) knob fresh ginger
2 Tbsp Chinese wine
2 tsp sesame oil
½ tsp Chinese five-spice powder
½ tsp salt
¼ tsp white pepper
2 egg-whites
1 tsp chilli oil
2 Tbsp finely chopped spring onion

Shell and de-vein the prawns. Cut in half, lengthways, and arrange on a heatproof plate. Cut the ginger into julienne strips and place on top of the prawns. Sprinkle the Chinese wine and sesame oil on top and season with the five-spice powder, salt and pepper. Beat the egg-whites lightly and pour over the prawns. Boil a little water in the bottom of a wok and place the prawns on a wooden rack above the level of the water. Place a tightly fitting lid on the wok and steam for 5-6 minutes. Before serving, sprinkle a little chilli oil over the prawns and garnish with finely chopped spring onions.

SESAME PRAWNS

12 king prawns
15 mm (³/₄ inch) knob fresh ginger
1 fresh red chilli
1 clove garlic
1 spring onion
2 Tbsp light soya sauce
75 ml (3 fl oz) Chinese wine
1 tsp sugar
¹/₄ tsp white pepper
1 egg
2 Tbsp milk
100 g (4 oz) plain flour
100 g (4 oz) sesame seeds
oil for deep-frying

Shell and de-vein the prawns but leave the tails intact. Cut half-way through the prawn and open out into a butterfly style. Shred the ginger and finely chop the chilli, spring onion and garlic and mix with soya sauce and wine. Add the sugar and pepper and pour the mixture over the prawns, then set aside for 15 minutes. Beat the egg lightly and mix with milk. Dip the prawns into the egg wash, dust with flour and coat with the sesame seeds. Heat the oil in a wok until very hot and deep-fry the prawns until golden brown. Drain and serve.

PRAWN CUTLETS

12 fresh king prawns
salt
freshly ground black pepper
2 Tbsp Chinese wine
3 Tbsp cornflour
4 eggs
100 g (4 oz) fine breadcrumbs

Shell and de-vein the prawns leaving the tails intact. Slice half-way through the prawns and open out in butterfly style. Season with salt and pepper and sprinkle on the Chinese wine. Set aside for 10 minutes. Beat the eggs and mix thoroughly with the cornflour. Dip the prawns into the mixture, and coat with breadcrumbs. Heat the oil in the wok until it starts to smoke, then deep-fry with the prawns until golden brown and cooked, approximately 2-3 minutes.

Sesame Prawns and Prawn Cutlets

STIR-FRIED SHRIMPS WITH TOMATO

450g (1 lb) fresh shrimps
1 egg-white
2 Tbsp Chinese wine
2 Tbsp cornflour
¹/₂ tsp salt
¹/₄ tsp pepper
4 medium sized tomatoes
2 spring onions
15mm (³/₄ inch) knob fresh ginger
1 clove garlic
3 Tbsp vegetable oil
1 Tbsp tomato sauce
2 Tbsp light soya sauce
1 tsp sugar
1 tsp vinegar
250ml (9 fl oz) chicken stock
2 tsp finely chopped coriander

Shell and de-vein the shrimps and place in a shallow dish. Season with salt and pepper. Lightly beat the egg-white with half the cornflour and half the Chinese wine and pour over the shrimps, then set aside for 15 minutes. Cut the tomato into wedges, cut the spring onion into 25mm (1 inch) lengths, chop the ginger and crush the garlic. Bring a pan of water to the boil and add the tomato. Cook for 1 minute, then remove, rinse and peel. Heat half the oil in a saucepan, add the ginger and garlic and stir-fry for 1 minute, then add the tomato, tomato sauce, soya sauce, sugar, vinegar, and chicken stock and bring to the boil. Mix the remaining cornflour with a small quantity of cold water and stir into the sauce. Allow to simmer for 2 minutes then remove from heat. Heat the remaining oil in a wok, add the shrimps and stir fry for 1 minute. Then pour in the sauce and remaining Chinese wine and cook for a further 2 minutes. Transfer to a serving dish and sprinkle with coriander.

SHRIMPS IN HOT GARLIC SAUCE

450 g (1 lb) fresh shrimps
1 egg-white
1 Tbsp cornflour
2 Tbsp Chinese wine
¹/₂ tsp salt
¹/₄ tsp white pepper
1 small brown onion
2 spring onions
3 fresh red chillies
1 fresh green chilli
25 mm (1 inch) knob fresh ginger
3 cloves garlic
600 ml (1 pint) peanut oil
1 Tbsp black bean paste
2 Tbsp light soya sauce
1 tsp sugar
125 ml (4 fl oz) clear fish stock
¹/₂ tsp sesame oil

Shell and de-vein the shrimps, leaving the tails intact, then cut in half lengthways. In a bowl whisk the egg-white with 2 tsp cornflour, add the wine, salt and pepper and stir well. Add the shrimps, stir to coat evenly and set aside for 30 minutes. Chop finely the onions, chillies and ginger and crush the garlic. Heat 550 ml (18 fl oz) of oil until it starts to smoke, then spoon in the coated shrimps. Stir-fry for 1 minute, then remove and drain on kitchen paper. Discard the cooking oil, add the fresh oil to the wok and place over a moderate heat. Add the onions, chilli, ginger and garlic and stir-fry for a further minute, then add the bean paste, soya sauce and sugar and mix well. Increase the heat, add the shrimps and continue to cook for a further minute, stirring frequently. Mix the remaining cornflour with a small quantity of stock, add to the wok together with the remaining stock and bring to the boil. Stir until the mixture thickens, then add the sesame oil and transfer to a serving dish.

MUSSELS IN BLACK BEAN SAUCE

2 kilos (4 1/2 lbs) fresh mussels
125 ml (4 fl oz) vegetable oil
3 Tbsp fermented black beans
1 small green pepper
3 fresh red chillies
25mm (1 inch) knob fresh ginger
2 cloves garlic
2 Tbsp sugar
1/2 tsp salt
1/4 tsp black pepper
225 ml (8 fl oz) chicken stock
1 Tbsp cornflour
freshly chopped parsley

Wash the mussels under cold running water and scrub with a stiff brush. Leave to soak in cold water for 20 minutes, then rub dry. Heat half the oil in a wok and stir fry the mussels until the shells open, discarding any that fail to do so. Set the mussels aside and clean the pan. Crush the soya beans and mix with a little cold water. Cut the green pepper, red chillies and ginger into thin strips and crush the garlic. Heat the remaining oil in the pan and stir-fry the garlic for 2 minutes. Add the soya bean, green pepper, chilli and ginger and continue to cook over a moderate heat for a further 2 minutes. Add the mussels, sugar, salt and pepper and pour in the chicken stock. Bring to the boil, then lower heat and simmer for 2 minutes. Mix the cornflour with a small quantity of cold water, add to the pan and stir until the sauce thickens slightly. Serve in individual clay pots and garnish with chopped parsley.

STIR- FRIED SCALLOPS

375 g (12 oz) fresh scallops
75 g (3 oz) dried black fungus
(wun yee)
3 chicken livers
4 tinned water chestnuts
20 mm (3/4 inch) knob fresh ginger
1 clove garlic
2 Tbsp peanut oil
2 Tbsp Chinese wine
4 Tbsp chicken stock
1 Tbsp light soya sauce
1 tsp dark soya sauce
1/2 tsp sesame oil
1 tsp sugar
1 Tbsp cornflour
sprigs of fresh coriander

Wash the scallops under cold running water and pat dry, then cut them horizontally into slices. Soak the fungus in warm water for 15 minutes. Slice the chicken livers. Slice the water chestnuts and chop finely the ginger and garlic. Heat the oil in a wok and stir-fry the scallops and chicken liver over a high heat for 1 minute, then remove and drain on kitchen paper. Add the ginger and garlic to the wok and stir-fry for 1 minute, then add the water chestnut and fungus and continue to cook for a further minute, stirring frequently. Add wine, stock, soya sauce, sesame oil and sugar and bring to the boil, then lower heat, return the scallops and cook for 30 seconds. Mix the cornflour with a small quantity of cold water and stir into the sauce, then transfer to a serving dish and garnish with fresh sprigs of coriander.

SPICY STEAMED POMFRET

1 whole pomfret
¹/₂ tsp salt
¹/₄ tsp white pepper
3 spring onions
2 fresh red chillies
1 clove garlic
20 mm (³/₄ inch) knob fresh ginger
2 Tbsp fermented black beans
¹/₄ tsp mustard powder
2 Tbsp Chinese wine
2 Tbsp light soya sauce
75 ml (3 fl oz) peanut oil
2 tsp finely-chopped coriander

Prepare the fish and make a number of incisions along each side. Rub the salt and pepper into the fish and set aside for 15 minutes. Slice the spring onions and place in a shallow heat-proof dish, then lay the fish on top. Finely chop the chilli, garlic and ginger and place in a mixing bowl, together with the black beans, mustard, wine and soya sauce. Mix well, then pour over the fish and place in a steamer. Steam over rapidly boiling water for 7-8 minutes, then remove and transfer the fish to a serving plate. Finally, heat
the peanut oil and pour over the fish, then sprinkle the finely-chopped coriander on top.

SMOKED POMFRET

1 pomfret, approximately 675 g
(1¹/₂ lbs)
25 mm (1 inch) knob fresh ginger
3 spring onions
2 Tbsp Chinese wine
2 Tbsp light soya sauce
1 tsp anise powder
1 tsp sugar
170 g (6 oz) rice
75 g (3 oz) plain flour
3 Tbsp dried tea leaves
2 tsp sesame oil

Clean the fish and, with a sharp knife, score in a criss cross fashion along both sides. Chop the ginger and spring onion very finely and mix half of this with the Chinese wine and soya sauce. Rub the mixture into the flesh of the fish and allow to stand for 30 minutes, then place in a steamer and cook for 5 minutes. Mix together the remaining ginger and spring onion, anise powder, sugar, rice, flour and tea leaves. Place the mixture into a wok and cook over a high heat. When it starts to smoke, place the fish on a perforated rack into the wok (and above the mixture). Cover the wok with a tightly-fitting lid and smoke for approximately 2 minutes. Transfer to a serving dish, sprinkle with hot sesame oil and garnish with sprigs of Chinese parsley.

Note: The fish in the picture is a decorated with a 'net' made from a large carrot. This is just one example of the fine vegetable carvings that play a major part in the presentation of Chinese food in many of the finer restaurants.

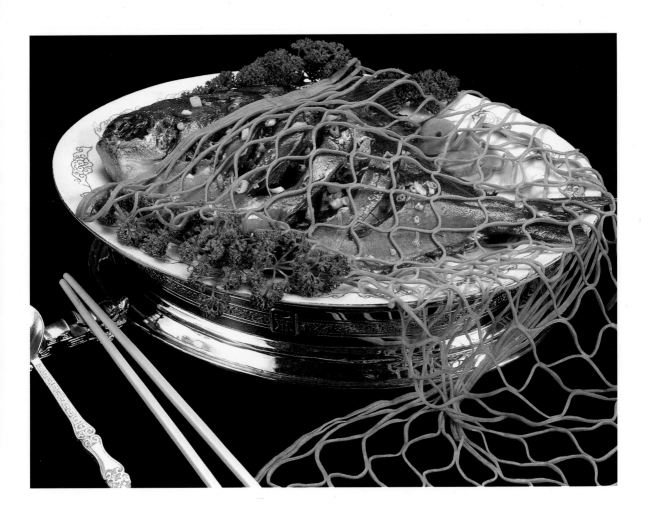

SWEET & SOUR FRIED FISH

1 pomfret, approx 675 g (1¼ lbs)
½ tsp salt
¼ tsp white pepper
1 egg
1 Tbsp cornflour
oil for deep-frying

Sauce:
1 small brown onion
1 small green pepper
2 fresh red chillies
20 mm (¾ inch) knob fresh ginger
1 clove garlic
125 g (4 oz) tin pineapple chunks
1 Tbsp peanut oil
2 Tbsp Chinese wine
2 Tbsp light soya sauce
2 Tbsp vinegar
125 ml (4 fl oz) fish or
chicken stock
4 Tbsp sugar
3 tsp cornflour

Clean and prepare the fish, leaving the head and tail intact. Score the skin in several places and rub in the salt and pepper. Whisk the egg with the cornflour and use to coat the fish on both sides, then set aside for 20 minutes. Heat the oil in a large wok until it starts to smoke, then reduce to a moderate heat, add the fish and deep-fry for 5 minutes until cooked and the skin is golden and crispy. Remove fish and drain on kitchen paper, then transfer to a serving dish and pour the sauce on top.

To make the sauce; chop coarsely the onion and green pepper and chop finely the chillies, ginger and garlic. Drain the pineapple chunks and reserve 2 Tbsp of juice. Heat the oil in a wok, add the onion, green pepper, chilli, ginger and garlic and stir-fry for 2 minutes, then add the wine, soya sauce, vinegar, stock, sugar and pineapple chunks. Bring to the boil and stir until the sugar is dissolved, then lower heat and allow to simmer for a further minute. Mix the cornflour with the reserved pineapple juice and stir in to the sauce to thicken slightly.

WEST LAKE FISH

900 g (2 lb) carp
3 spring onions
1 large brown onion
1 red pepper
1 green pepper
25 mm (1 inch) knob fresh ginger
2 cloves garlic
3 lettuce leaves
4 Tbsp vegetable oil
2 Tbsp Chinese wine
1 tsp sesame oil
2 Tbsp vinegar
2 Tbsp tomato sauce
2 tsp sugar
1 tsp cornflour
salt
freshly ground black pepper

Clean and scale the fish, leaving the head and tail intact. Make six slits along the back of the fish. Chop the spring onion, brown onion, red and green peppers and ginger, crush the garlic and shred the lettuce leaves. Heat half the vegetable oil in a wok and stir-fry the spring onion, pepper, ginger and garlic for 3-4 minutes, then add the wine, sesame oil and 1 litre (2¼ pints) of water and bring to the boil. Place the fish in the boiling liquid, cover the wok with a tightly-fitting lid and cook for 2 minutes. Remove from the heat and allow to stand for a further 15 minutes, then transfer the fish and vegetables to a serving dish. Heat the remaining oil in a clean pan, add the brown onion and stir-fry for 3 minutes then add the vinegar, sugar and tomato sauce and season to taste with salt and pepper. Mix the cornflour with a small quantity of cold water and add to the pan together with the shredded lettuce. Stir well, cook for a further minute, then spoon over the fish.

STEAMED GAROUPA WITH HAM

675 g (1¹/₂ lbs) garoupa fillets
10 dried Chinese mushrooms
75 g (3 oz) sliced Chinese ham
5 spring onions
75 ml (3 fl oz) vegetable oil
10 small pieces kale (or broccoli)
¹/₄ tsp salt
1 tsp ground ginger
1 Tbsp Chinese wine
100 ml (4 fl oz) chicken stock
2 tsp sesame oil
freshly ground white pepper
1¹/₂ Tbsp cornflour

Cut the fish, diagonally, into slices about 15 mm (¹/₂ inch) thick. Soak the mushrooms in warm water for 30 minutes, then squeeze dry, discard the hard stems and halve the caps. Cut the ham into thin strips and soak in warm water for 15 minutes. Slice the spring onions and place on the bottom of a shallow oven-proof dish, then arrange alternating slices of fish, ham and mushroom on top. Set the dish on a bamboo rack, place in a steamer and cook for 5 minutes. Meanwhile, heat half the vegetable oil in a wok and stir-fry the kale for 1 minute, then add 100 ml (4 fl oz) of cold water, season with salt and bring to the boil. Cook for 3 minutes, then remove the kale, drain well and keep warm. Heat the remaining vegetable oil in a clean wok, add the ginger and stir-fry for 1 minute, then add the wine, stock and sesame oil and season with pepper. Bring to the boil and allow to simmer for 1 minute. Mix the cornflour with a small quantity of cold water and stir into the sauce to thicken slightly. To serve; remove the dish from the steamer, arrange the kale around the edge and pour the wine sauce on top.

Poultry

Poultry plays a prominent role in the Chinese diet and features in all the regional cuisines. However the methods of cooking vary greatly, from diced chicken meat mixed with nuts and vegetables, or minced pigeon served in lettuce leaves, to the legendary Beggar's Chicken and, perhaps the most universally famous and popular Chinese dish of all, Peking Duck. Various game birds are available according to seasons but, as in the West, their stronger flavours tend to make them popular only with a minority.

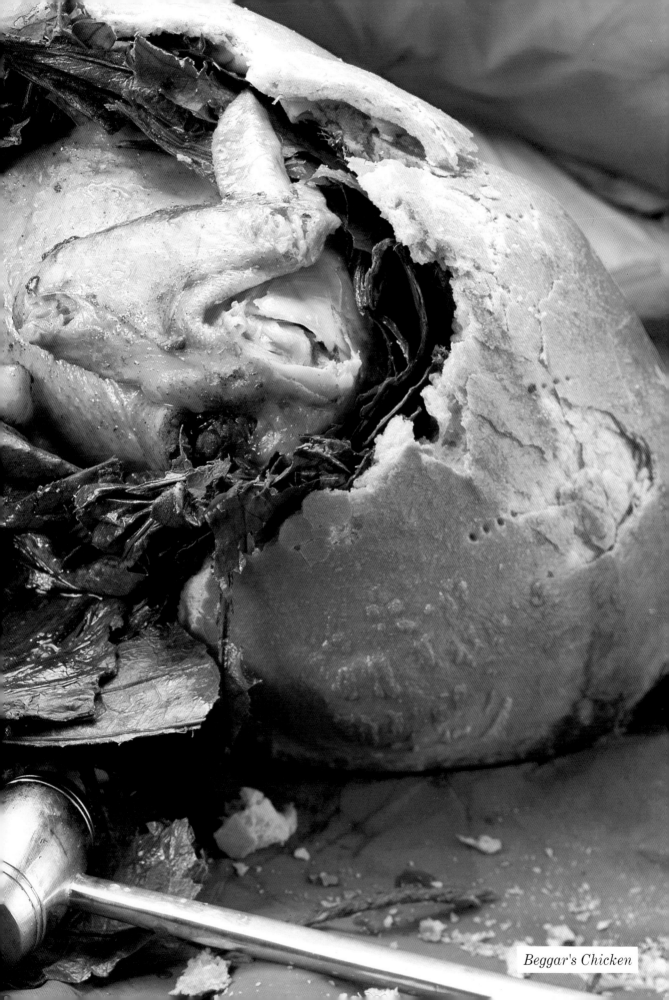

Beggar's Chicken

BEGGAR'S CHICKEN

1 chicken,
approx 1.5 kilos (3¼ lbs)
2 tsp salt
6 dried Chinese mushrooms
150 g (5 oz) pork
75 g (3 oz) pickled cabbage
75 g (3 oz) beetroot
1 large brown onion
1 spring onion
15 mm (½ inch) knob fresh ginger
2 Tbsp light soya sauce
1 tsp dark soya sauce
2 Tbsp Chinese wine
1 tsp sesame oil
freshly ground black pepper
lotus leaves*
450 g (1 lb) shortcrust pastry
dough

Clean and prepare the chicken and rub inside and out with the salt. Soak the mushrooms in warm water for 30 minutes, then drain, discard the hard stems and shred the caps finely. Shred the pork, cabbage and beetroot and chop the onions and ginger. Season with soya sauce, Chinese wine, sesame oil and freshly ground black pepper and stir over medium heat for 2-3 minutes. Remove mixture from the wok, drain off any excess oil and stuff inside the chicken. Wrap the stuffed chicken in lotus leaves and completely seal with the pastry dough. Bake in a very hot oven for 1½ hours, then reduce heat and continue cooking for a further 45 minutes. To serve break away the pastry and remove the lotus leaves.

Note: Traditionally the chicken is enclosed in clay rather than pastry but the latter is simpler and more usually acceptable for the domestic kitchen. *Also note that if lotus leaves are not readily available they may be omitted when using pastry although this will most certainly result in some loss of the original flavour.

DICED CHICKEN WITH WALNUTS

400 g (14 oz) chicken meat
1 egg-white
3 Tbsp light soya sauce
¼ tsp white pepper
2 Tbsp cornflour
500 ml (18 fl oz) peanut oil
100 g (4 oz) shelled walnuts
1 green pepper
1 spring onion
15 mm (½ inch) knob fresh ginger
1 clove garlic
1 Tbsp dark soya sauce
3 Tbsp Chinese wine
1 Tbsp vinegar
4 Tbsp chicken stock
2 tsp sugar

Cut the chicken into small dice and place in a shallow bowl. Whisk together the egg-white, light soya sauce, pepper and half the cornflour and pour over the chicken. Stir to coat the chicken evenly and set aside for 30 minutes. Heat 450 ml (16 fl oz) of oil and fry the walnuts over a low heat until golden brown, then drain and set aside. Dice the green pepper, chop the spring onion and ginger and crush the garlic. Heat the remaining oil in a wok and stir-fry the chicken for 1 minute, then remove and drain on kitchen paper. Add the green pepper, onion, ginger and garlic to the wok and stir-fry for 1 minute, then replace the chicken, add the dark soya sauce, wine, vinegar, stock and sugar and bring to the boil. Lower heat and cook for 2 minutes, then mix the remaining cornflour with a small quantity of cold water and stir in until the sauce thickens slightly. Adjust seasonings to taste, then remove the wok from the heat, add the walnuts and stir to mix thoroughly.

CHICKEN BAKED IN SALT

1 chicken, approx 1.25 kilos (2³/4 lbs)
1 shallot
2 spring onions
1 clove garlic
15 mm (¹/2 inch) knob fresh ginger
2 Tbsp Chinese wine
2 Tbsp light soya sauce
2 tsp dark soya sauce
¹/4 tsp white pepper
¹/4 tsp anise powder
3 kilos rock salt

Clean and prepare the chicken. Finely chop the shallot, spring onions, garlic and ginger and place in a bowl. Add the wine, soya sauce, pepper and anise powder and mix thoroughly. Rub the outside of the chicken with the mixture and stuff the remainder inside. Set aside for 45 minutes, then wrap in ovenproof paper. Heat the rock salt in a large wok until it is very hot, then pour half into another heated wok, place the chicken on top and cover with remaining rock salt. Cover with a tightly fitting lid and leave for 6 minutes. Then, remove the chicken, reheat the salt and repeat the cooking process. Do this a further three times so that the chicken will have had a total cooking time of 30 minutes. To serve, remove the paper and chop the chicken into small pieces.

SMOKED CHICKEN

1 chicken, approx 1.5 kilos (3¹/2 lbs)
2 tsp salt
¹/2 tsp white pepper
¹/2 tsp anise powder
20 mm (³/4 inch) fresh ginger
2 spring onions
1 Tbsp Chinese wine
2 Tbsp light soya sauce
2 Tbsp sesame oil
75 g (3 oz) black tea leaves
2 Tbsp sawdust
2 Tbsp brown sugar

Clean and prepare the chicken. Mix together the salt, pepper and anise powder and rub evenly over the inside and outside of the chicken then set aside for 2 hours. Chop the ginger and spring onions, mix with the wine and stuff inside the chicken. Steam the chicken for 20 minutes, then allow to cool and rub the outside with half the soya sauce and sesame oil. Mix together the tea leaves, sawdust and sugar and place in the bottom of a large wok. Arrange the chicken on a rack which fits in the wok and leave at least a 50 mm (2 inch) clearance between the chicken and the tea leaves. Light the tea leaves, place a cover on the wok and smoke for 6 minutes, then remove the chicken and coat with the remaining soya sauce and sesame oil. Return to the rack and smoke for a further 10-12 minutes, until the skin turns brown. Allow to cool then cut into bite-size pieces and transfer to a serving dish.

DRUNKEN CHICKEN

*1 young chicken, approx 1.25 kilos
(2¹/₂ lbs)
20 mm (³/₄ inch) knob fresh ginger
2 spring onions
900 ml (1¹/₂ pints) chicken stock
1 tsp salt
¹/₂ tsp white pepper
300 ml (10 fl oz) Chinese wine*

Prepare the chicken and place in a large pan. Slice the ginger and spring onions and add to the pan. Pour in the stock and bring to the boil, then reduce heat and simmer for 20-25 minutes. Remove the chicken, cut into serving-size pieces and arrange in a shallow dish. Season with salt and pepper, then combine 175 ml (6 fl oz) of the stock with the wine and pour over the chicken. Cover the dish with foil and place in the refrigerator for 36 hours, turning the chicken occasionally. Serve cold.

CHICKEN BUNDLES

4 chicken breasts
2 Tbsp light soya sauce
¹/₂ tsp sesame oil
¹/₂ tsp sugar
¹/₄ tsp freshly ground black pepper
2 tsp cornflour
4 dried Chinese mushrooms
100 g (4 oz) roasted pork fillet
2 hard-boiled eggs
200 g (7 oz) Chinese cabbage
1 Tbsp Chinese wine
1 Tbsp oyster sauce
2 tsp cornflour

Cut the chicken into slices, about 15 mm (¹/₂ inch) thick. Sprinkle the soya sauce, sesame oil, sugar, pepper and cornflour over the chicken and set aside for 20 minutes. Soak the mushrooms in warm water for 30 minutes, then discard the hard stems and cut the caps into sticks. Slice the pork into similar sticks and cut each egg into 8 pieces. Bring a pan of salted water to the boil and blanch the cabbage for 4-5 minutes. Drain the cabbage and cut leaves into strips approximately 120 mm × 30 mm (5 inch × 1¹/₄ inch). On to each strip place a piece of chicken, mushroom, pork and egg, then fold into secure bundles. Arrange the bundles on an ovenproof plate, place in a steamer and cook over rapidly boiling water for 8-10 minutes, then transfer to a serving dish and pour the liquid from the cooking plate into a small pan. Mix the cornflour with 1 Tbsp of cold water and add to the pan together with the wine and oyster sauce. Bring to the boil and stir well, then pour over the chicken bundles and serve immediately.

PEKING DUCK

1 fat duck, approx 2.5 kilos
(5¹/₂ lbs)
1 Tbsp salt
2 tsp Chinese five-spice powder
125 g (4 fl oz) golden syrup
2 Tbsp honey
2 Tbsp light soya sauce
6 spring onions
1 small cucumber
plum sauce

Pancakes:
500 g (1 lb 2 oz) plain flour
¹/₄ tsp salt
400 ml (14 fl oz) boiling water

Clean and prepare the duck. Cut off the feet but leave the head. Immerse the duck into a pan of rapidly boiling water for just a few seconds then dry thoroughly. Rub the salt and five-spice powder inside the duck. Mix the syrup, honey and soya sauce with a small quantity of cold water and bring to the boil. Coat the duck, both inside and out, with the hot syrup mixture, place a string around the neck and hang in a cool, draughty place for 4-5 hours. (If preferred an electric fan may be used to stretch the skin more quickly). Afterwards place the duck in a moderately hot oven for approximately 1³/₄ hours, turning occasionally to ensure a crisp, golden skin all over. To serve; carve off pieces of skin and arrange on a serving plate. Cut the spring onions into 5 cm (2 inch) lengths and the cucumber into thin sticks. Place these on the table together with a bowl of plum sauce and a plate of pancakes. To eat; place a piece of duck on a pancake, add a piece of spring onion and cucumber and top with some plum sauce. Fold the sides of the pancake over the filling and tuck in the ends to form a secure roll.

To make the pancakes; sift the flour and salt into a mixing bowl and make a well in the centre. Pour in the boiling water a little at a time and gradually mix into the flour to form a soft dough. Knead gently for 10 minutes until the dough becomes pliable, then cover and allow to stand for 20 minutes. Roll into a cylindrical shape approximately 5 cm (2 inch) in diameter and cut into circles, approximately 5 mm (¹/₄ inch) thick. Brush one side of each circle with sesame oil and place together with the oiled sides facing, then roll each out until approximately 15 cm (6 inch) in diameter. Heat a heavy pan and cook each pair of pancakes for approximately 1 minute, turning to cook on both sides. When cooked peel the pancakes apart and stack on a warm plate.

Note: As only the outside of the duck is carved for serving with the pancakes, quite a lot of meat remains on the bones. This should be cut off, shredded or chopped and stir-fried with vegetables. The carcass is then left for preparation of a delicious soup.

ONION DUCK

1 duckling, approx 1.5 kilos (3¼ lbs)
2 large brown onions
2 spring onions
2 Tbsp light soya sauce
2 tsp dark soya sauce
freshly ground black pepper
100 ml (4 fl oz) vegetable oil
250 ml (9 fl oz) chicken stock
2 Tbsp Chinese wine
2 tsp brown sugar
2 Tbsp cornflour

Clean and prepare the duck. Chop the onions and spring onions and place in a mixing bowl. Add the soya sauce and pepper and mix well, then stuff inside the duck and secure with twine. Heat the oil in a wok and fry the duck over a moderate heat for 10-12 minutes, turning occasionally to ensure the skin is evenly browned. Remove the duck and drain on kitchen paper. Pour the stock into a large saucepan together with an equal quantity of cold water. Place the duck in the pan and bring to the boil, then reduce the heat and add the wine and sugar. Cover the pan and simmer for approximately 1¼ hours until the duck is tender, then remove, cut into serving-size pieces and arrange on a serving dish. Bring the stock back to the boil, adjust seasonings to taste and reduce by half. Mix the cornflour with a small quantity of cold water and add to the pan. Reduce heat and stir for 1-2 minutes, then pour over the duck and serve immediately.

SPICEY GOOSE

3 kilos (6½ lb) goose
25 mm (1 inch) knob fresh ginger
6 cloves garlic
4 spring onions
4 sprigs fresh coriander
1 cinnamon stick
10 Szechuan peppercorns
2 Tbsp sugar
1 tsp salt
¼ tsp anise powder
4 Tbsp dark soya sauce
2 Tbsp oyster sauce
3 Tbsp Chinese wine

Clean the goose and pat dry. Bring 2 litres of water to the boil in a wok, then remove from heat. Plunge the goose into the water and leave for 3 minutes, then remove and hang to dry. Empty the wok of water, then add the goose and all the ingredients except the oyster sauce and 1 Tbsp Chinese wine. Add enough water to cover the whole bird and bring to the boil. Cover the wok and cook over moderate heat for 1 hour. Remove the goose, then strain the stock into a bowl and set aside for making the sauce. Place the goose on a rack and steam for another hour until very tender (a chopstick will pierce the meat easily). Then, chop the goose into bite-size pieces, arrange on a serving platter and serve with the sauce.

To make the sauce; Reduce the stock by half, then add the oyster sauce and remaining wine, and stir to blend.

NB: This dish can also be served cold.

BAKED STUFFED PIGEONS

4 pigeons
1 tsp salt
½ tsp Chinese five-spice powder
freshly ground black pepper
6 dried Chinese mushrooms
100 g (4 oz) fresh shrimps
75g (3 oz) lean pork
2 large brown onions
2 cloves garlic
25mm (1 inch) knob fresh ginger
2 spring onions
75 g (3 oz) bamboo shoot
2 Tbsp vegetable oil
2 eggs
2 Tbsp light soya sauce
2 tsp dark soya sauce
2 Tbsp Chinese wine
2 Tbsp oyster sauce
2 tsp cornflour
100 g (4 oz) butter

To prepare the pigeons; cut along the back-bone, remove the carcass and spread the birds open. Season the insides with salt, five-spice powder and freshly ground black pepper. Soak the mushrooms in warm water for 30 minutes then discard the hard stems. Shell and de-vein the shrimps and chop into small pieces. Chop finely the pork, mushroom caps, brown onions, garlic, ginger, spring onions and bamboo shoots. Heat the oil in a wok, add the chopped shrimps, pork and vegetables and stir-fry for 3-4 minutes. Remove, drain off excess oil, then pass the mixture through a mincer and place in a mixing bowl. Beat the eggs lightly, then add to the mixture together with the soya sauce, Chinese wine, oyster sauce and cornflour. Stir to blend thoroughly, then spread the mixture evenly over the inside of the pigeons. Re-shape the birds and secure with strips of heat-proof parchment paper. Heat the butter in a clean wok and when it starts to 'sizzle' add the pigeons and cook for 4-5 minutes, turning frequently to ensure the skin is evenly golden and crispy. Finally, place a lid on the pan, lower heat and cook fairly slowly until the birds are tender. Check during the later stage, and add a little more butter if necessary.

Note: If preferred, the final stage of cooking may be done in a steamer, but be sure to brown the birds in butter first.

PIGEON WITH BAMBOO SHOOTS

350 g (12 oz) pigeon meat
½ tsp salt
¼ tsp black pepper
½ tsp sugar
¼ tsp meat tenderizer
3 dried Chinese mushrooms
100 g (4 oz) bamboo shoots
3 Tbsp vegetable oil
2 Tbsp Chinese wine
2 tsp light soya sauce
1 tsp dark soya sauce
2 tsp oyster sauce
1 Tbsp cornflour
2 tsp sesame oil

Cut the pigeon meat into small, thin slices, season with salt, freshly ground black pepper, sugar and meat tenderizer and allow to stand for 30 minutes. Soak the mushrooms in warm water for 40 minutes, discard the hard stems and cut the caps into thin slices. Cover the bamboo shoots with cold water, bring to the boil, cook for 3-4 minutes, then drain and cut into small pieces. Heat the oil in a wok and stir-fry the pigeon for 5 minutes, turning occasionally, then remove and set aside. Pour off most of the oil from the wok, add the mushroom and bamboo shoot and stir for 30 seconds. Then, replace the pigeon, add the Chinese wine, chicken stock, soya sauce and oyster sauce and continue to cook for a further 3 minutes. Mix the cornflour with a small quantity of cold water, add to the pan and stir until the sauce thickens, then transfer to a serving dish. Finally, warm the sesame oil and sprinkle over the pigeon.

Meats

Pork and beef (in that order) are the most popular meats eaten by the Chinese. Veal is never found and recipes calling for lamb generally originate only from the Northern frontier regions. The meat is usually cut into small pieces; chopped, sliced or shredded, then often marinated with soya sauce, ginger juice and Chinese wine before being cooked, together with a variety of vegetables, for a minimum amount of time.

Shredded Beef in Taro Nest

SHREDDED BEEF IN TARO NEST

300g (10 oz) lean beef
1/2 tsp salt
1/4 tsp white pepper
2 Tbsp Chinese wine
1 brown onion
1 green pepper
25mm (1 inch) knob fresh ginger
2 fresh red chillies
2 cloves garlic
350 g (12 oz) taro root
1 egg
3 Tbsp cornflour
oil for deep-frying
1 tsp sugar
2 Tbsp light soya sauce
2 tsp oyster sauce
3 Tbsp beef stock

Cut the beef into fine shreds and place in a shallow dish. Season with the salt, pepper and wine and set aside for 20 minutes. Shred the onion, pepper and ginger, chop the chilli and crush the garlic. Cut the taro into fine shreds and place in a dish. Beat the egg with half the cornflour and pour over the taro. Mix well, then arrange between two rounded wire baskets. Heat the oil in a large wok until it starts to smoke, then submerge the baskets and deep-fry the taro for 3-4 minutes until set into the shape of a nest, then remove and drain on kitchen paper. Pour away all but 3 Tbsp of oil from the wok, add the beef and stir-fry over a high heat for 1 minute, then remove and set aside. Add the onion, green pepper, ginger, chilli and garlic and stir-fry for 2-3 minutes, then replace the beef, add the sugar, soya sauce, oyster sauce and stock and bring to the boil. Reduce the heat and cook over a moderate heat for a further 2 minutes. Mix the remaining cornflour with a small quantity of cold water and stir into the beef. To serve; arrange the taro nest on a plate and fill with the beef.

Note: Potatoes may be substituted for taro root.

SPICED BEEF & BEAN CURD

300 g (10 oz) lean beef
1 Tbsp Chinese wine
2 tsp dark soya sauce
1/4 tsp salt
1/4 tsp white pepper
125 g (4 oz) fresh beancurd
2 shallots
3 fresh red chillies
25 mm (1 inch) knob fresh ginger
2 cloves garlic
1 Tbsp fermented black beans
125 ml (4 fl oz) vegetable oil
75 ml (3 fl oz) beef stock
1 Tbsp oyster sauce
1 Tbsp chilli sauce
2 tsp cornflour
1 tsp sesame oil
1 Tbsp chopped spring onion

Mince the beef, mix with the wine, dark soya sauce, salt and pepper and set aside for 20 minutes. Cut the beancurd into small cubes. Chop the shallots, chillies and ginger and crush the garlic. Heat the oil in a wok, add the beancurd and deep-fry over a high heat for 2-3 minutes. Remove the beancurd and drain on kitchen paper. Pour off all but 2 Tbsp of oil. Place the ginger and garlic in the wok and stir-fry for 1 minute, then add the beef, shallot, chilli and black beans and continue to stir over a fairly high heat for 2 minutes. Add the stock, oyster sauce and chilli sauce and bring to the boil, then reduce the heat and cook slowly for a further 2 minutes. Mix the cornflour with a small quantity of water, add to the wok and stir for 1 minute, then return the beancurd, sprinkle in the seasame oil and adjust seasoning to taste. Stir until the beancurd is heated through, then transfer to a serving dish and garnish with chopped spring onion.

SLICED BEEF WITH CRISPY BATTER

250 g (8 oz) lean beef
2 Tbsp cornflour
2 tsp Chinese wine
¼ tsp salt
¼ tsp white pepper
100 g (4 oz) crispy fried batter
15 mm (½ inch) knob fresh ginger
2 spring onions
4 Tbsp peanut oil
1 egg
1 Tbsp light soya sauce
1 tsp dark soya sauce
½ tsp sugar
75 ml (3 fl oz) beef stock
½ tsp sesame oil
chopped spring onions

Cut the beef into small thin slices and place in a shallow dish. Dust with half the cornflour, sprinkle the wine on top and season with salt and pepper. Set aside for 30 minutes. Chop the crispy batter into small cubes, shred the ginger and cut the spring onions into 25 mm (1 inch) lengths. Heat the oil in a wok and stir-fry the beef over a moderate heat for 1 minute, then remove and drain. Reheat the oil, add the ginger and spring onion and cook for 2 minutes, stirring frequently. Break the egg into a bowl and whisk lightly, then add the soya sauce, sugar and stock and pour into the wok. Bring to the boil, stir in the sesame oil and replace the beef. Mix the remaining cornflour with a small quantity of cold water and add to the wok, then add the crispy batter and heat through. Allow to simmer for a final 2 minutes, then transfer to a serving dish and garnish with spring onions.

BEEF WITH PEPPERS & PINE NUTS

450g (1 lb) sirloin steak
1 Tbsp Chinese wine
2 Tbsp light soya sauce
1 Tbsp ginger juice
1 tsp sugar
2 Tbsp cornflour
1 red pepper
1 green pepper
20mm (¾ inch) knob fresh ginger
3 cloves garlic
300ml (10 fl oz) vegetable oil
75g (3 oz) pine nuts
2 Tbsp oyster sauce
300ml (10 fl oz) chicken stock
salt to taste
freshly ground black pepper

Cut the sirloin into small cubes and place in a shallow dish. Mix together the soya sauce, wine, ginger juice, sugar and half the cornflour and pour over the beef, then set aside for 30 minutes. Cut the red and green peppers into small squares, chop the ginger and crush the garlic. Heat 1 tablespoon of oil in a wok and stir-fry the red and green peppers for 1 minute, then remove and set aside. Pour the remaining oil into the pan and fry the pine nuts until they turn slightly yellow, then remove and set aside. Add the beef to the same pan, stir well and cook for 20 seconds then drain and set aside. Pour off most of the oil from the wok, add the garlic and ginger and stir-fry for 1 minute, then replace the beef and cook over a very high heat for a further 20 seconds. Then, add the red and green pepper and stir well. Add the oyster sauce and chicken stock and bring to the boil. Season with salt and pepper, add the pine nuts and mix well. Finally, mix the remaining cornflour with a small quantity of cold water and stir into the sauce to thicken slightly.

MONGOLIAN BEEF

350g (12oz) lean beef
1 egg
2 tsp cornflour
salt
freshly ground black pepper
2 carrots
1 small green pepper
15mm (3/4 inch) knob of fresh
ginger
2 red chillies
2 cloves garlic
oil for deep frying
75g (3oz) rice noodles
1 Tbsp Chinese wine
1 Tbsp light soya sauce
1 tsp sugar
2 Tbsp finely chopped spring onion

Cut the beef into thin slices and place in a shallow dish. Beat the egg and combine with the cornflour, salt and pepper and 1 Tbsp of water. Pour over the meat then set aside for one hour. Heat the oil in a wok until very hot and deep fry the noodles until they puff-up, then remove, drain and place on a serving plate. Re-heat the oil, add the beef and stir-fry until half cooked, then add the carrot and green pepper and continue to cook for a further minute. Then, remove and drain the meat and vegetables and pour away most of the oil. Re-heat the pan, add the ginger, chilli and garlic and stir-fry for 1 minute, then add the wine, soya sauce and sugar and stir well. Replace the meat and vegetables, adjust seasonings to taste and cook for a further 2 minutes. To serve, transfer to the bed of noodles and garnish with finely chopped spring onions.

BRAISED BEEF & TURNIPS

700 g (1 ¹/₂ lbs) topside
¹/₂ tsp salt
¹/₄ tsp white pepper
400 g (14 oz) turnips
20 mm (³/₄ inch) knob fresh ginger
2 cloves garlic
3 Tbsp vegetable oil
1 Tbsp soya bean paste
1 Tbsp Chinese wine
1 Tbsp light soya sauce
2 tsp dark soya sauce
1 Tbsp oyster sauce
1 tsp sugar
2 tsp cornflour

Cut the beef into large chunks and season with salt and pepper. Cut the turnips into bite-size wedges, slice the ginger and crush the garlic. Heat half the oil in a wok, add the beef and stir-fry for 2 minutes to seal completely, then remove the beef and set aside. Heat the remaining oil in a clay cooking pot, add the ginger, garlic and soya bean paste and stir-fry for 3-4 minutes, then add the beef and cook over a high heat for a further 2 minutes, stirring frequently. Add sufficient water to barely cover the beef and place a tightly-fitting lid on the pot. Lower heat and allow to cook slowly for 1¹/₂ hours, then remove the lid, bring back to a rapid boil and add the wine, soya sauce, oyster sauce, sugar and turnips. Again, lower the heat, adjust seasonings to taste and allow to simmer for a further 15 minutes. Finally, mix the cornflour with a small quantity of cold water and stir into the sauce to thicken slightly, then serve immediately.

SPARERIBS WITH BLACK BEANS

550 g (1¼ lbs) pork spareribs
½ tsp salt
freshly ground black pepper
3 Tbsp fermented black beans
3 fresh red chillies
2 fresh green chillies
1 small green pepper
25 mm (1 inch) knob fresh ginger
1 carrot
1 clove garlic
3 Tbsp vegetable oil
2 tsp sugar
2 Tbsp light soya sauce
1 tsp dark soya sauce
1 tsp sesame oil
2 Tbsp Chinese wine

Chop the ribs into 40 mm (1½ inch) lengths and season with salt and pepper. Mash the black beans with a fork. Chop the chillies and green pepper, slice the ginger and carrot and crush the garlic. Heat the oil in a wok, add the spareribs and stir-fry for 2 minutes, then add the black beans, ginger and garlic and continue to cook over a moderate heat for a further 3 minutes, stirring frequently. Add the sugar and 100 ml (4 fl oz) of water and bring to the boil, then reduce the heat and cover with a tightly fitting lid. Cook for 5 minutes, then remove the lid, add the chillies, green pepper and carrot, increase the heat and cook for a further 3 minutes, stirring frequently. Add the soya sauce and sesame oil, stir to heat through, then add the wine and transfer to a serving dish.

SWEET & SOUR PORK

450g (1 lb) fillet of pork
2 Tbsp cornflour
2 Tbsp Chinese wine
1 Tbsp light soya sauce
1/2 tsp salt
1/2 tsp white pepper
1 tsp white sugar
1 fresh red chilli
1 fresh green pepper
1 clove garlic
15mm (3/4 inch) knob fresh ginger
30g (10 oz) diced pineapple
3 Tbsp vinegar
2 Tbsp brown sugar
1 Tbsp tomato sauce
1 tsp dark soya sauce
25ml (4 fl oz) chicken stock
oil for frying

Cut the pork into bite-sized pieces and place in a shallow dish. Mix one third of the cornflour with half the wine, the light soya sauce, salt, pepper, and white sugar. Pour this mixture over the meat and set aside for 30 minutes. Cut the green pepper into small pieces, chop the chilli and ginger and crush the garlic. Heat the oil in a wok until it starts to smoke, then add the pork, lower the heat and fry for 2 minutes. Remove, drain and set aside. Heat the vinegar in a clean wok, add the brown sugar and stir until completely dissolved, then add the tomato sauce, chicken stock and remaining soya sauce and bring to the boil. Lower heat and allow to simmer for 2 minutes, then set aside. Heat 1 tablespoon of oil in a separate wok, add the pepper, chilli, ginger and garlic and stir-fry over high heat for 1 minute. Replace the pork, add the pineapple, the remaining wine and sauce and bring to the boil. Adjust seasonings to taste, stir well and cook for a further 30 seconds then transfer to a serving plate. Garnish with sprigs of fresh coriander.

PORK FILLET WITH LEMON SAUCE

8 pork loin fillets
1/4 tsp salt
1/4 tsp white pepper
4 egg yolks
2 Tbsp light soya sauce
2 Tbsp Chinese wine
75g (3oz) cornflour
oil for deep frying
fresh lemon slices

Lemon sauce:
2 Tbsp butter
2 Tbsp plain flour
75ml (3 fl oz) fresh lemon juice
75ml (3 fl oz) chicken stock
2 Tbsp Chinese wine
2 tsp dark soya sauce
2 tsp sugar
salt to taste
freshly ground black pepper
2 tsp cornflour

Lay the fillets in a shallow dish and season with salt and pepper. Beat the egg yolks and mix with the soya sauce, wine and one-third of the cornflour. Pour the mixture over the pork and set aside for 30 minutes, then dust the pork with the remaining cornflour. Heat the oil in the wok until it starts to smoke, then deep fry the pork until it is tender, golden and crispy. Remove from the oil, drain thoroughly and arrange on a serving plate, then pour on the sauce and garnish with slices of fresh lemon.

To make the sauce: melt the butter in a saucepan, add the flour and stir to blend. Retain over a moderate heat, add the lemon juice and stock and bring to the boil. Add the wine, soya sauce and sugar and season to taste with salt and pepper. Stir to blend thoroughly and cook for a further minute. Finally, mix the cornflour with a small quantity of cold water and stir into the sauce to thicken slightly.

PORK WITH STRAW MUSHROOMS

450g (1 lb pork) tenderloin
225g (8oz) tinned straw
mushrooms
2 Tbsp Chinese wine
1 Tbsp light soya sauce
1/2 tsp salt
1/2 tsp white pepper
2 Tbsp cornflour
15mm (3/4 inch) knob fresh ginger
2 cloves garlic
3 Tbsp peanut oil
3 Tbsp chicken stock
1 Tbsp oyster sauce
2 Tbsp finely chopped spring
onions.

Slice the pork diagonally, then pound until quite thin and place into a shallow dish. Mix soya sauce with half the Chinese wine and half the cornflour, add the salt and pepper and pour over the pork. Cut the straw mushrooms in half, blanch in boiling water for 30 seconds then drain and set aside. Heat two-thirds of oil in a pan and fry the pork until golden brown on both sides, then remove and set aside. Clean the pan, heat the remaining oil, add the ginger and garlic and stir fry for 2-3 minutes. Replace the pork and add the mushrooms, then cook over a high heat for 1 minute. Add the stock, oyster sauce and remaining wine and mix well. Mix the remaining cornflour with a small quantity of cold water, and add to the sauce to thicken slightly. Continue to cook for a further minute, stirring frequently, then transfer to a serving dish and garnish with spring onions.

Pork Fillet with Lemon Sauce

FRIED PORK WITH VEGETABLES

300 g (10 oz) lean pork
¼ tsp salt
¼ tsp white pepper
¼ tsp Chinese five-spice powder
1 egg
1 brown onion
1 green pepper
2 tomatoes
2 fresh red chillies
25 mm (1 inch) knob fresh ginger
1 clove garlic
3 Tbsp breadcrumbs
2 Tbsp vegetable oil
3 Tbsp chicken stock
1 Tbsp Chinese wine
2 tsp dark soya sauce
2 tsp cornflour
1 tsp sesame oil
1 Tbsp finely chopped spring onion

Cut the pork and season with salt, pepper and five-spice powder. Beat the egg lightly and pour over the pork, then set aside for 20 minutes. Slice the onion, chop the green pepper, tomatoes, chillies and ginger and crush the garlic. Remove the pork from the marinade and coat with breadcrumbs. Heat the oil in a wok until it starts to smoke then add the pork and fry for 2-3 minutes, turning so that both sides are golden brown. Remove and drain on kitchen paper. Add the onion and garlic to the wok and cook for 2 minutes, then add the green pepper, tomato, chilli and ginger and stir-fry for a further 2 minutes. Add the stock, wine and soya sauce and bring to the boil, then replace the pork and cook over a moderate heat for 2-3 minutes. Mix the cornflour with a small quantity of cold water and stir into the mixture, then transfer to a serving dish. Heat the sesame oil and sprinkle over the pork, then finally garnish with the finely chopped spring onion.

PORK & BEAN SPROUTS

300 g (10 oz) lean pork
1 egg
2 Tbsp Chinese wine
2 tsp light soya sauce
1 tsp sugar
¼ tsp white pepper
2 tsp cornflour
2 dried Chinese mushrooms
150 g (6 oz) bean sprouts
2 spring onions
1 clove garlic
4 Tbsp peanut oil

Cut the pork into fine shreds and place in a shallow dish. Whisk the egg lightly and mix with half the wine, the soya sauce, sugar, pepper and cornflour, then pour over the pork and set aside for 45 minutes. Soak the mushrooms in warm water for 30 minutes, then discard the hard stems. Blanch the bean sprouts in boiling water for 1 minute, then drain thoroughly. Chop the mushrooms and spring onions and crush the garlic. Heat the oil in a wok until it starts to smoke, then add the pork and stir-fry for 30-45 seconds. Remove the pork and drain on kitchen paper. Pour away most of the oil. Place the garlic in the wok and stir-fry for 1 minute, then replace the pork together with the bean sprouts, mushroom and spring onions. Sprinkle on the remaining wine, adjust seasonings to taste and cook over a high heat for a further 1-2 minutes, stirring frequently.

DEEP-FRIED LEG OF LAMB

1.25 kilos (2½ lbs) boned leg of
lamb
20 mm (¾ inch) knob fresh ginger
3 cloves garlic
10 Szechuan peppercorns
½ tsp anise powder
1 Tbsp sugar
2 tsp salt
2 Tbsp light soy sauce
2 tsp dark soy sauce
1 Tbsp vinegar
2 eggs
3 Tbsp cornflour
peanut oil for deep-frying

Dip:
2 Tbsp fresh lemon juice
2 tsp salt
1 Tbsp sugar
2 Tbsp light soy sauce
1 Tbsp dark soy sauce
3 Tbsp water
1 tsp finely chopped red chilli
1 tsp shredded fresh coriander

Chop the lamb into bite-size cubes, place in a wok and cover with water. Bring to the boil and simmer for 3 minutes then remove and rinse under cold running water. Slice the ginger and crush the garlic. Replace the meat in the wok, add the ginger, garlic and peppercorns and cover with water approximately 25 mm (1 inch) above the meat. Bring to the boil and add the anise powder, sugar, salt, soya sauce and vinegar and stir well. Cook over a moderate heat until the meat is tender, then remove and set aside in a shallow dish. Whisk the egg lightly with the cornflour, pour over the meat and stir to coat evenly. Finally, heat the oil in a wok and deep-fry the meat until golden and crispy. Remove, drain off excess oil and serve with prepared dip.

To make the dip; Mix together all the ingredients and stir until blended.

STIR-FRIED LAMB WITH GINGER

450 g (1 lb) fillet of lamb
1 tsp salt
½ tsp white pepper
3 Tbsp Chinese wine
1 Tbsp fresh lemon juice
2 Tbsp light soya sauce
1 tsp sesame oil
2 tsp sugar
1 Tbsp cornflour
4 spring onions
25 mm (1 inch) knob fresh ginger
1 fresh red chilli
2 cloves garlic
225 ml (8 fl oz) peanut oil

Cut lamb into small thin slices, place in a shallow dish and season with salt and pepper. Mix together 2 Tbsp wine, the lemon juice, soya sauce, sesame oil, sugar and cornflour and pour over the meat. Stir to coat evenly and set aside for 30 minutes. Cut the spring onion into short lengths, slice the ginger, shred the chilli and crush the garlic. Heat all but 1 Tbsp of the oil in a wok until almost smoking and add the lamb. Cook until the colour changes, then remove and drain off excess oil. Clean the wok, add the remaining oil and stir-fry the ginger for 30 seconds, then add the chilli and garlic and continue to stir for a further minute. Replace the lamb, add the spring onion and stir-fry over a high heat until the lamb is heated through. Then, remove from the heat, sprinkle the remaining wine over the lamb and transfer to a serving plate.

Vegetables

Many main dishes of fish, poultry and meat will already include vegetables but, nevertheless, a well-balanced Chinese meal will nearly always include a vegetable dish in its own right. Whether stir-fried or boiled the actual cooking time is minimal so the original texture and natural goodness of the vegetables are retained. Some local vegetables may be difficult to find outside Asian markets so improvisation may be necessary and local seasonal vegetables should always take priority when planning a meal.

Clay Pot Vegetable Casserole

CLAY POT VEGETABLE CASSEROLE

6 dried Chinese mushrooms
75 g (3 oz) tinned straw
mushrooms
75 g (3 oz) mung bean noodles
125 g (4 oz) string beans
250 g (9 oz) Chinese cabbage
1 small eggplant
20 mm (3/4 inch) knob fresh ginger
1 clove garlic
100 g (4 oz) fried beancurd
300 ml (10 oz) peanut oil
450 ml (15 fl oz) chicken stock
1 Tbsp light soya sauce
2 Tbsp oyster sauce
1/2 tsp sesame oil
2 Tbsp cornflour
1 tsp Chinese wine

Soak the mushrooms in warm water for 30 minutes, then discard the hard stems and halve the caps. Blanch the straw mushrooms in boiling water for 1 minute, then drain. Soak the noodles in warm water for 10 minutes, then drain and rinse under cold running water. Top and tail the beans and cut in half. Cut the cabbage into large chunks and slice the eggplant. Slice the ginger and chop the garlic. Cut the beancurd into small cubes. Heat the oil in a large clay pot, add the mushrooms, beans, cabbage and eggplant and stir-fry for 1 minute, then remove with a slotted spoon and drain on kitchen paper. Pour off all but 2 Tbsp of oil and replace the pot over a moderate heat. Add the ginger and garlic and stir-fry for 1 minute, stirring frequently. Return the vegetables to the pot and stir well, then add the stock, soya sauce, oyster sauce and sesame oil and bring to the boil. Reduce the heat, place the noodles and beancurd on top, cover the pot and simmer for 5 minutes. Mix the cornflour with a small quantity of cold water and stir into the stock to thicken slightly, then adjust seasonings to taste, sprinkle the wine on top and serve directly from the pot.

CABBAGE & WATER CHESTNUTS

450 g (1 lb) Chinese cabbage
75 g (3 oz) tinned straw
mushrooms
100 g (4 oz) tinned water chestnuts
15 mm (1/2 inch) knob fresh ginger
1 clove garlic
75 ml (3 fl oz) vegetable oil
400 ml (14 fl oz) chicken stock
salt to taste
freshly ground black pepper
1 tsp sugar
2 Tbsp Chinese wine
2 Tbsp oyster sauce
2 tsp cornflour

Discard the hard stem and outside leaves from the cabbage and cut into serving-size pieces. Blanch in boiling water for 2 minutes, then drain and set aside. Blanch the mushrooms and chestnuts for 1 minute, then drain. Slice the chestnuts, chop the ginger very finely and crush the garlic. Heat two thirds of the oil in a wok until fairly hot then fry the mushrooms and cabbage for 1 minute. Remove and drain on kitchen paper. Reheat the oil, add the chestnuts and fry for 3-4 minutes until they turn golden brown. Remove the chestnuts and drain on kitchen paper and discard the oil. Return the vegetables to the wok, add three-quarters of the stock, the salt, pepper and sugar and bring to the boil. Reduce the heat, cover and let simmer for 8-10 minutes, then remove and drain. Wipe the wok, add the remaining oil and stir-fry the ginger and garlic over a fairly high heat for 2 minutes then add the wine and remaining stock and bring to the boil. Return the vegetables and add the oyster sauce. Mix the cornflour with a small quantity of cold water and stir in to the sauce to thicken slightly, then transfer to a serving dish.

VEGETARIAN STEW

8 dried Chinese mushrooms
75 g (3 oz) dried black fungus
(wun yee)
1 brown onion
2 carrots
125 g (4 oz) kale
75 g (3 oz) tinned bamboo shoot
75 g (3 oz) tinned water chestnuts
75 g (3 oz) tinned straw
mushrooms
100 g (4 oz) fresh beancurd
2 Tbsp vegetable oil
2 Tbsp light soya sauce
4 Tbsp chopped crispy fried batter
10 gingko nuts
2 tsp sesame oil
1 Tbsp cornflour

Soak the dried mushrooms in warm water for 30 minutes and discard the hard stems. Retain 125 ml (4 fl oz) of the water. Soak the fungus in warm water for 30 minutes, then drain and cut into narrow strips. Chop the onion, carrots and kale and slice the bamboo shoot and chestnuts. Cut the beancurd into small cubes. Heat the oil in a wok, add the mushrooms and beancurd and stir-fry for 3 minutes, then add three-quarters of the reserved water and soya sauce and bring to the boil. Reduce heat and let simmer for 4-5 minutes, then add all the vegetables and the remaining water. Bring back to the boil, add the fried batter, gingko nuts and sesame oil and adjust seasonings to taste. Reduce the heat and let simmer for 5 minutes, then add the strips of fungus and cook for a further minute. Finally, mix the cornflour with a small quantity of cold water and stir into the vegetables. Transfer to a large dish and serve immediately.

BRAISED VEGETABLES IN WINE

225 g (8 oz) broccoli spears
1 whole lettuce
300 ml (10 fl oz) vegetable oil
600 ml (1 pint) chicken stock
2 Tbsp peanut oil
1 tsp crushed garlic
2 Tbsp Chinese wine
2 Tbsp oyster sauce
1 Tbsp light soya sauce
1 tsp dark soya sauce
1 Tbsp cornflour
2 Tbsp finely chopped ham

Wash the vegetables under cold running water and tear off the lettuce leaves. Dry thoroughly. Heat the vegetable oil in a wok and fry the broccoli for 2 minutes, then remove and drain. Pour the stock into a saucepan and bring to the boil. Reduce heat, add the broccoli and simmer for 2 minutes, then remove, drain thoroughly and place in a serving dish. Bring back to the boil, add the lettuce and cook for 1 minute, then remove and arrange on top of the broccoli. Meanwhile, heat the peanut oil in a clean wok and stir-fry the garlic for 1 minute, then add the wine, oyster sauce and stock and bring to the boil. Mix the cornflour with a small quantity of cold water and add to the sauce. Reduce heat and simmer until the sauce thickens, then pour over the vegetables and sprinkle the chopped ham on top.

DRY FRIED BEANS

450 g (1 lb) green beans
75 g (3 oz) shrimps
1 clove garlic
15 mm (¹/₂ inch) knob fresh ginger
75 g (3 oz) pickled vegetables
75 g (3 oz) minced pork
oil for deep frying
3 Tbsp chicken stock
1 Tbsp light soya sauce
1 Tbsp sugar
freshly ground black pepper
2 tsp vinegar
1 tsp sesame oil
freshly sliced red chilli

Top and tail the beans and cut into 60 mm (2¹/₂ inch) lengths. Shell and de-vein the shrimps and chop finely. Crush the garlic and chop the ginger and pickled vegetables. Heat the oil in a wok until it starts to smoke then deep-fry the beans for 2-3 minutes, until they start to 'wrinkle'. Then, remove the beans, drain on kitchen paper and pour the oil from the wok. Place the wok back on the heat, add the beans and stir-fry until they start to blacken, then remove and set aside. Pour 2 Tbsp of oil into the wok, reheat, add the shrimp, garlic, ginger, pickles and pork and stir-fry for 2 minutes then add the stock, soya sauce, sugar and pepper and bring to the boil. Add the beans and stir over a high heat until the liquid has evaporated, then stir in the vinegar and sesame oil and transfer to a serving dish. Garnish with freshly sliced red chilli.

STUFFED MUSHROOMS

12 dried Chinese mushrooms
200g (7 oz) shrimps
1 tsp salt
¹/₂ tsp white pepper
2 tsp Chinese wine
1 tsp sesame oil
1 tsp cornflour
2 Tbsp finely chopped ham

Soak the mushrooms in warm water for 40 minutes, then remove the hard stems. Shell and de-vein the shrimps and chop finely. Mix the shrimp together with salt, pepper, sesame oil, wine and cornflour and pound to produce a smooth, sticky paste. Spread the paste on the underside of the mushrooms and sprinkle with chopped ham. Place the mushrooms on a rack, cover and steam for approximately 20 minutes, then transfer to a serving plate and sprinkle a little finely chopped coriander on top of each mushroom.

Sweet Flavours

With Chinese meals, simple or formal, at home or in a restaurant, elaborate dessert dishes do not play such an important role as they do in the West. This is particularly true of Cantonese cuisine, where the meal is usually completed with fresh fruit or a simple fruit-based dish requiring little preparation. Not surprisingly, what hot and filling sweet dishes there are have mostly originated in the Northern and Western regions where the weather is considerably colder than in the South.

甜品

Almond Jelly & Fruit Salad

ALMOND JELLY & FRUIT SALAD

2 Tbsp agar agar powder
75 g (3 oz) sugar
1 tsp almond essence
150 ml (6 fl oz) sweet
condensed milk
300 g (10 oz) tin fruit salad

Place 600 ml (1 pint) of water in a saucepan, add the agar agar and half the sugar and bring to the boil. Lower the heat and simmer for 10 minutes, then add the almond essence, condensed milk and remaining sugar and continue to cook for a further 5 minutes, stirring occasionally. Pour the mixture into a shallow, lightly-greased cake tin, allow to cool, then refrigerate to set firmly. To serve; cut the jelly into small cubes and place in a serving bowl together with the fruit salad and shaved ice.

TOFFEE APPLES

3 large apples
100 g (4 oz) plain flour
vegetable oil for deep-frying
100 ml (4 fl oz) peanut oil
150 g (5 oz) sugar
2 Tbsp sesame seeds
iced water

Peel and core the apples and cut into wedges. Mix the flour with sufficient cold water to produce a fairly thick smooth batter. Dip the pieces of apple in the batter to coat evenly. Heat the vegetable oil in a wok and deep-fry the apple for 2-3 minutes until golden brown, then remove from the oil and drain on kitchen paper. Pour the peanut oil into a saucepan, add the sugar and 3 Tbsp of cold water and bring to the boil. Stir over a moderate heat until the sugar has completely dissolved, then add the pieces of apple. Stir to coat evenly, then remove the apple, sprinkle with sesame seeds and plunge immediately into the iced water so that the syrup sets hard.

CANDIED YAM

225 g (8 oz) yam
100 g (4 oz) sugar
2 tsp fresh lemon juice
1 tsp grated orange peel
peanut oil for deep-frying
1 tsp sesame seeds

Cut the yam into 15 mm (^{1}/$_2$ inch) cubes and place in a saucepan. Cover with cold water and bring to the boil. Cook for 3 minutes, then pour off all but 3 Tbsp of water, add the sugar and lemon juice and bring back to the boil. Add the orange peel, reduce the heat and stiry until the sugar has caramelised, then remove, cut into pieces and allow to cool. Then, heat the peanut oil in a wok until it is almost smoking and deep-fry the pieces of candied yam for 1-2 minutes. Finally, remove with a slotted spoon, drain off the excess oil and coat with sesame seeds.

Sweet Bean Paste Meringue

5 egg-whites
75 g (3 oz) custard powder
3 Tbsp sugar
1/4 tsp red food colouring
125 g (4 oz) sweet bean paste
2 Tbsp cornflour
oil for deep-frying

Beat the egg-whites until fairly stiff, then add the custard powder, blend thoroughly and continue to beat until a very stiff consistency results. In a shallow dish, mix the sugar with just sufficient colouring to turn it deep pink, then set this to one side. Mix the bean paste with a small quantity of cold water and shape into small balls. Dust these with cornflour and dip into the egg mixture, allowing a considerable amount to stick; the finished meringue should be approximately 50 mm (2 inches) in diameter. Heat the oil in a wok until it starts to smoke and deep-fry the meringues until the outsides are golden, approximately 2 minutes, then remove, drain off excess oil and roll in the coloured sugar. Serve immediately.

Date Pancakes

150 g (5 oz) pitted dates
150 g (5 oz) granulated sugar
100 g (4 oz) sweet bean paste
525 ml (18 fl oz) peanut oil
egg-wash
3 Tbsp powdered sugar

Pancakes:
150 g (5 oz) plain flour
2 Tbsp milk
2 eggs
2 Tbsp soft butter
1 tsp sugar

Chop the dates into tiny pieces and place in a saucepan together with the sugar. Add just sufficient cold water to cover and bring to the boil. Lower heat and allow to simmer for 5 minutes, stirring frequently. Allow the mixture to cool, then press through a fine sieve and combine with the bean paste. Heat 2 Tbsp of oil in a wok and stir-fry the mixture over a low heat for 3 minutes, then remove and drain off excess oil. Spoon portions of the mixture on to the pancakes, fold up securely and brush with the egg-wash. Heat the remaining oil in the wok until very hot (almost smoking) then add the pancakes, lower the heat, and deep-fry until the outsides are golden. Finally, remove from the oil with a slotted spoon, drain on kitchen paper and dust with the powdered sugar. Serve immediately.

Glossary

In editing the foregoing recipes the aim has been to list ingredients generally familiar and readily available worldwide. The following notes, therefore, are intended to give some simple and useful information on Chinese culinary terms rather than act as a comprehensive glossary to this book.

ABALONE

A large sea mollusc with a particularly hard shell, often seen in fish tanks outside Chinese restaurants. Fresh abalone can be very expensive but the canned variety is readily available.

BAK CHOI

Chinese white cabbage with a mild, yet distinctive flavour. It's often added to soups and meat dishes as well as being served as a separate vegetable.

BAMBOO SHOOTS

A cream-coloured conical shaped vegetable used frequently in Chinese cooking. When bought fresh they must be peeled to remove the hard skin, then boiled for some considerable time. It's much simpler to buy the canned variety which are readily available and, which unlike many other vegetables, retain the fresh flavour.

BEAN CURD

Soya beans treated with an extract of rennet. Sold fresh in slabs, it is highly nutritious and often used in Chinese cooking.

BEAN PASTE

Made with a base of preserved soya beans (see below) and available in various forms. Hot bean paste, used a lot in Northern Chinese cooking, is flavoured with chillies, while other varieties use sugar and seasonings.

BEAN SPROUTS

The sprouts of the green mung bean can be bought fresh in Asian provision stores and many Western supermarkets. They require a minimum amount of cooking time and should always be 'crispy' when served. When used in mixed dishes they should be one of the last ingredients added.

CHILLIES

Fresh chillies are used liberally in some styles of Chinese cuisine, especially in dishes from the north and the western province of Szechuan. Regardless of the quantity suggested in any recipe, the preference of personal palates must always be the main consideration. Fresh chillies are generally chopped or sliced before cooking and the seeds are often removed. Dried chillies are sometimes used whole for cooking and discarded before serving.

CHINESE MUSHROOMS

Dried black mushrooms have a unique flavour for which there is no substitute. First soaked in warm water, the hard stems are discarded and the caps used in many soups and mixed dishes as well as being served as a separate vegetable. They are an essential ingredient in any Chinese kitchen and are readily available in all Asian provision stores.

CHOI SUM

One of the most popular Chinese vegetables. It has round green stems, 'pencil-like' leaves and small yellow flowers. It has a slightly bitter taste and is often served with oyster sauce (see below).

CORIANDER

Also known as Chinese parsley, the seeds have an aromatic flavour and are readily available whole or ground. The leaves are used in cooking and as a garnish and can often be found in a dried form in well-stocked Asian provision stores. Western parsley is, at best, a very poor substitute.

DIM SUM

A collective name for savoury and sweet Chinese snacks, normally served from breakfast through lunch but also popular with afternoon tea. There are literally hundreds of varieties and, as most people like to try as many as possible, it is a complicated and time-consuming meal to prepare. For that reason it's more likely to be served in a restaurant than at home.

CHINESE FIVE-SPICE POWDER

A strong seasoning made from grinding together equal quantities of fennel seeds, cinnamon bark, cloves, star anise and Szechuan peppercorns (see below). Can be stored for long periods in an air-tight container.

GINGER

A root stem with a very pungent flavour. It has a rough, thin skin which should be peeled off before using. Sliced, chopped or grated it adds a distinctive 'spice' to a dish. The commercially packaged powdered ginger has a quite different taste and is not a suitable substitute.

HOI SIN SAUCE

A sweet, spicy sauce made from soya beans, chillies, garlic, spices and sugar. Often served as a dip with meat and poultry dishes.

OYSTER-SAUCE

Made from oysters boiled in salted water and soya sauce, it's readily available and will keep for long periods. It's used to add a delicious 'extra' flavour to many dishes, particularly meats and vegetables.

SOYA SAUCE

The best known of all Chinese sauce and an indispensible ingredient in every kitchen both for use in cooking and for serving as a dip. It comes in various grades and the finest, and most concentrated, can be quite expensive. The dark sauce is only used in cooking.

WATER CHESTNUTS

Actually not a nut but a bulb. They have very tough skins which have to be removed if using fresh. Best to buy the canned variety which will keep for a month after opening if covered with fresh water (changed daily) and refrigerated.

WOK

A half-spherical shaped cooking utensil used in all Chinese kitchens. It can be used for stir-frying, deep frying, stewing and steaming and is probably the most practical and versatile kitchen utensil ever invented. A valuable addition to even the most well-equipped western kitchen.

WON TON WRAPPERS

Squares of very thin noodle pastry available fresh or frozen at Chinese grocery stores and some western supermarkets.

YAM

A root vegetable with a mild, slightly sweet flavour. Boiled and mashed is often used for desserts.

Index